The Arts and State Governments

At Arm's Length or Arm in Arm?

Julia F. Lowell
Elizabeth Heneghan Ondaatje

Commissioned by

The research in this report was produced within RAND Education, a unit of the RAND Corporation. The research was commissioned by The Wallace Foundation as part of its State Arts Partnerships for Cultural Participation (START) initiative, which was designed to help state arts agencies develop more-effective strategies for encouraging arts participation in their states.

Library of Congress Cataloging-in-Publication Data

Lowell, Julia, 1961-
   The arts and state governments : at arm's length or arm in arm? / Julia F. Lowell, Elizabeth Heneghan Ondaatje.
      p. cm.
   "MG-359."
   Includes bibliographical references.
   ISBN 0-8330-3867-2 (pbk. : alk. paper)
   1. Government aid to the arts—United States—Case studies. 2. Art commissions—United States. 3. U.S. states—Cultural policy.
   I. Ondaatje, Elizabeth Heneghan. II. Title.

NX740.L67 2006
700.79'73—dc22
                                                                2006009929

The RAND Corporation is a nonprofit research organization providing objective analysis and effective solutions that address the challenges facing the public and private sectors around the world. RAND's publications do not necessarily reflect the opinions of its research clients and sponsors.

RAND® is a registered trademark.

Cover design by Eileen Delson La Russo

Published 2006 by the RAND Corporation
1776 Main Street, P.O. Box 2138, Santa Monica, CA 90407-2138
1200 South Hayes Street, Arlington, VA 22202-5050
4570 Fifth Avenue, Suite 600, Pittsburgh, PA 15213
RAND URL: http://www.rand.org/
To order RAND documents or to obtain additional information, contact
Distribution Services: Telephone: (310) 451-7002;
Fax: (310) 451-6915; Email: order@rand.org

Preface

Almost half of all U.S. public-sector grants to the arts are provided by state arts agencies (SAAs), which, as government organizations, derive most of their authority and much of their funding from elected officials. During the 1990s, many SAA leaders discovered that the position of their agencies on the margins of state government was not serving them well. Support for the arts was not high on the list of governmental priorities, and the growth of SAA budgets had stalled.

In this report, the authors adopt a public-management framework to examine SAA leaders' efforts to more firmly establish their agencies as valued and integral units of state government. Case studies of two SAAs, the Montana Arts Council and the Maine Arts Commission, are used to illustrate public management principles and to clarify some of the risks and rewards of bringing the arts and political worlds closer together.

This is the second in a series of publications reporting the findings of a multi-year RAND Corporation study of the changing roles and missions of SAAs. The first report—*State Arts Agencies 1965–2003: Whose Interests to Serve?*—broadly describes how SAAs have evolved in response to changes in their political and cultural environments. Future reports will continue to explore efforts by SAAs to adapt their missions, roles, and structures to American economic, political, and cultural realities of the 21st century.

This report was produced within RAND Education, a division of the RAND Corporation. The research was made possible by The Wallace Foundation as part of its State Arts Partnerships for Cultural Participation (START) initiative, which was designed to help SAAs develop more-effective strategies for encouraging arts participation in their states. The Wallace Foundation supports the development of knowledge from multiple sources and differing perspectives.

Contents

Figures

Summary

The U.S. system of state arts agencies (SAAs), conceived in the mid-1960s, was designed to increase local opportunities for state residents to participate in the arts, and to facilitate local control over public arts funding decisions. SAAs' primary strategy for achieving these goals has been to award grants to arts organizations and artists in their states. By many measures, this approach has been successful: Professional artists and arts organizations can be found throughout the country, and state and local arts agencies now control the bulk of public-sector grant monies dedicated to the arts.

However, as part of the political compromise that led to the creation of the National Endowment for the Arts (NEA), SAAs were also expected to generate a broad base of political support for public funding of the arts. In this they have been less successful: Even though a majority of Americans claim to support public funding of the arts, state government spending on the arts is minimal—and may be losing ground relative to other types of state expenditures. Perhaps more important, most SAAs have not succeeded in convincing state government leaders that the arts should be integral to their planning for the future of their states.

The research described in this report is part of a larger RAND Corporation study that explores the changing missions and roles of SAAs. The study has been funded by The Wallace Foundation as part of its State Arts Partnerships for Cultural Participation (START) initiative, which gave 13 SAAs multiyear grants in support of efforts to increase arts participation in their states. Drawing on a review of the data and literature on SAAs and the NEA, recent research on public administration, and in-depth interviews with SAA staff, board members, and grantees, we argue that SAAs' "arm's-length" approach to state government—which was intended to insulate arts grantmaking from possible political influence—has contributed to the marginalization of SAAs within state government.

A more strategic approach that reaches both outward to the public and upward toward government officials offers a promising alternative. Two case studies, one in Montana and one in Maine, offer examples of how SAA leaders are closing the gap between the arts world and the political world, overcoming budget and political crises and improving their ability to serve the residents of their states.

At Arm's Length

Following the example of the New York State Council on the Arts (and before that, the Arts Council of Great Britain), the early SAAs adopted two important organizational features: board-based governance and constituent-driven decisionmaking. SAAs are governed by boards of politically appointed volunteers who are authorized to set agency policies and allocate agency resources. Paid staff, led by executive directors, administer SAA programs and help their boards formulate policies. Volunteer panels of outside experts provide advice and recommendations.

SAAs were set up this way to ensure that arts grants would be awarded for artistic and technical merit rather than on the basis of political, ideological, or personal preferences of elected officials. In principle, board-governed agencies are better able than more traditional, hierarchical agencies to operate at arm's length from politics for four main reasons: board members are not paid, their terms of service are staggered, they are difficult to remove, and their decisionmaking is collective. Outside of budget actions and restrictive legislation, elected officials' means of influencing SAAs are limited. Instead, the decisions of SAAs are heavily influenced by their arts community constituents. Through mechanisms such as advisory panels, members of the arts community help determine SAA policies, design SAA programs, and decide individual grant awards.

But this relative insulation of SAAs from politics has come at a price. Their visibility within state government is low, and state political leaders appear not to understand how SAA programs and activities benefit those outside the arts community. Moreover, past strategies for protecting and growing SAA budgets appear to be losing their effectiveness. For example, the introduction of legislative term limits in many states has limited SAAs' ability to rely on legislative "arts champions" to protect their interests, major arts organizations are increasingly reluctant to lobby for their SAAs because state arts grants represent such a small percentage of their revenues, and statewide citizen advocacy groups have not been able to convince state officials that support for the arts should be a governmental priority.

Budgetary and Political Trends

It was not always this way. For the first 15 to 20 years after most SAAs were established, their low profile within state government did not seem to matter. Federal arts grants to the states grew strongly, and state legislative appropriations for SAAs grew even more strongly—although admittedly from a very low base. By 1985, federal spending on the NEA was exceeded by the states' total spending on their SAAs; and by 1994, 35 SAAs were receiving more than two-thirds of their total revenues from their own state legislatures. Further, state support during the 1980s grew more rapidly on average for the arts than for other categories of state general fund expenditures. State officials seemed content to let SAA budgets grow, to allow SAAs to manage their own affairs, and, in general, to treat them with benign indifference.

During the 1990s, however, these trends were broken. The NEA's budget was cut dramatically, with grim consequences for SAAs that still relied heavily on federal grants to fund their programs. To make things worse, a combination of economic recession, rapidly growing entitlement programs, and mounting voter resistance to tax increases began to squeeze state budgets significantly. And finally, movements to limit the size of government swept the country, movements demanding that government organizations at all levels provide acceptable justification for their activities or risk dramatic downsizing or elimination.

Given these developments, SAA leaders came to realize they must find new ways to demonstrate to state officials that their agencies are vital elements of state government—that is, that SAAs, through their support for the arts, help to meet states' priority needs. Two SAAs that have made significant moves in this direction are the Montana Arts Council and the Maine Arts Commission.

Case Studies

The Montana Arts Council and the Maine Arts Commission are not particularly representative SAAs. They are both small, independent agencies in rural states having no tradition of substantive government support for the arts. Nonetheless, they illustrate an evolution in thinking about mission, capacity, and especially relations with elected officials that is taking place in SAAs across the country. Both agencies have knocked down barriers between the arts world and the political world. In doing so, they appear not only to have stabilized their budgets, but also to have strengthened their legitimacy with government officials and the public.

Montana. In 1997, the Montana Arts Council faced what was probably the biggest crisis in its history. Inspired in part by U.S. congressional attempts to eliminate the NEA, a Montana state legislator gathered widespread support for a bill designed to eliminate the Council. His arguments emphasized fiscal conservatism, but he was supported by many people, both in the legislature and among the public, who held strong negative views of artists and the arts.

Council supporters responded quickly and strongly to this move to eliminate the agency. In a grassroots effort, hundreds of people throughout the state flooded legislators' offices with phone calls and faxes in support of the agency. But the real work began after the crisis was resolved and the agency's budget was (partially) restored. Council leaders concluded that their agency had become too isolated from ordinary Montanans and their elected representatives. They have now adopted a new and self-consciously strategic approach to their relationship with elected officials and the public, one that seeks to demonstrate the importance of the arts to ordinary Montanans. Working closely with statewide economic development and education groups, they are also emphasizing the practical benefits that can be achieved by public investment in the arts.

Maine. The crisis for the Maine Arts Commission centered on economics rather than values. Unlike the situation in Montana, no coordinated opposition saw support of the arts as an inappropriate use of taxpayer funds. Nevertheless, by the mid-1990s, the agency's prospects were bleak. Its NEA grant had been radically reduced, and state officials saw little room for the arts in an overburdened state budget. Within three years, the Commission had lost the bulk of its grantmaking funds.

As in Montana, agency leaders faced a crisis, in this case that they had almost no money to allocate to their arts-community constituents. Their response was, first, to canvas their state to determine what the Commission could still do that would be of value to Mainers. They then focused their funds in support of locally determined cultural needs—a solution that proved tremendously popular with elected officials as well as average citizens. They also decided to collaborate closely with other statewide cultural agencies, which added to their political support. In all, the Commission managed not only to recoup its budgetary losses within a few short years, but also, in the 2000s, to put the arts (and culture in general) at the center of governmental plans for revitalizing the state economy.

Closer Relations with Elected Officials

The Montana and Maine cases illustrate a principle emphasized in the recent literature on public administration: The most successful government agencies tend to be led by managers who are both entrepreneurial and politically responsive. A recognized leader in this field of research is Mark H. Moore, a professor at Harvard's Kennedy School of Government. In 2002, The Wallace Foundation invited Moore to introduce its 13 START grantees to concepts and tools he had developed for other federal, state, and local government agencies.

Moore (1995) suggests that government managers should judge for themselves what would be most valuable for their agencies to do, given their legislative mandates. In making their decisions, however, they should take into account the political expectations of their agencies (including the expectations of current constituents) and the resources available to them. This idea is captured by Moore's "strategic triangle" of issues:

- Public value;
- Legitimacy and support; and
- Operational capacity.

To create public value, government managers must identify a compelling mission for their agency. To mobilize legitimacy and support for that mission, managers must engage with elected officials. And finally, to ensure that the mission can be carried out, managers must conduct hardheaded calculations of what is operationally feasible.

Moore's triangle provides a useful lens for examining the SAA experiences in Montana and Maine. The two agencies' initial responses to their crises were not the same: Council leaders in Montana sought to build legitimacy and support for their current mission, whereas Commission leaders in Maine sought out a new and more compelling mission. At least in part, the differences in strategy may have arisen from agency leaders' perceptions about their operating capacity. Maine's budget cuts were severe enough to force a reexamination of the agency's mission; Montana's were not. Regardless, both strategies helped the agencies develop a closer relationship with elected officials.

Montana and Maine are not alone. Their efforts to mobilize legitimacy and support parallel those of many other SAAs. For example, several SAAs have taken steps in recent years to strengthen their boards, paying particular attention to the role of board members as advocates for the agency. Many are examining their programs and activities to identify how they may benefit a broad spectrum of state citizens and are seeking new ways to communicate those benefits to state political leaders. Finally, several SAAs are exploring how the arts can, in addition to being valuable in their own right, contribute to a state-determined public policy agenda. To what extent these agencies, and the arts community, actually allow their programs to be shaped by state government priorities remains to be seen.

Conclusion

There are risks, of course, to allowing elected officials a greater say in state arts policies and programs. One risk is that state arts grantmaking will become politicized, with legislators' biases, rather than legitimate policy concerns, driving individual grant awards. Another risk is that SAAs will become too closely associated with a particular set of public policy objectives and a particular group of elected officials, making them vulnerable when new objectives are introduced or new officials take office. Finally, there is the risk that policymakers may lose sight of what is uniquely valuable about the arts, judging state-supported arts activities only on the basis of their contributions to narrow, measurable outcomes such as the creation of jobs or the raising of educational test scores. If this happens, the arts may lose out to other state investments that promise greater or faster returns.

We believe that the potential rewards to "arm-in-arm" relations between SAAs and state governments are worth the risks. In particular, SAAs have much to gain by adopting a more strategic approach to public management, which calls for greater attention to the needs of the public and improved communication with elected officials. SAA managers who understand these constituencies can better determine how to use the resources at their disposal to create public value through the arts. They will also be in a better position to build alliances that help stabilize state arts funding and perhaps even increase it. Most important, if SAAs become fuller partners in state and local planning, the people of their states will benefit from increased engagement with the arts both now and in the future.

Acknowledgments

We received a number of thoughtful reviews of earlier drafts of this document, as well as many helpful suggestions based on oral presentations of the report's findings. We were also given a large amount of unpublished data, background materials, and information from individual state arts agencies and from the National Assembly of State Arts Agencies. For their help, we would particularly like to thank the following people (who, at the time, were affiliated with the institutions indicated): Shelley Cohn and Mollie Lakin-Hayes (Arizona Commission on the Arts), Paul Minicucci (California Arts Council), Mary Kelley (Massachusetts Cultural Council), Judith Rapanos (Michigan Council for Arts and Cultural Affairs), Robert Booker (Minnesota State Arts Board), Jonathan Katz and Kelly Barsdate (National Assembly of State Arts Agencies), Mary Regan and Vicki Vitiello (North Carolina Arts Council), Wayne Lawson and Gregg Dodd (Ohio Arts Council), Heather Doughty and Philip Horn (Pennsylvania Council on the Arts), Ricardo Hernandez (Texas Commission on the Arts), Michael Mclendon (Vanderbilt University), Alexander Aldrich (Vermont Arts Council), Kristin Tucker and Mark Gerth (Washington State Arts Commission), Anthony Radich (Western States Arts Federation), and George Tzougros (Wisconsin Arts Board).

A very special thanks is due to Arlynn Fishbaugh and Cinda Holt of the Montana Arts Council and to Alden Wilson and Bryan Knicely of the Maine Arts Commission, all of whom not only spent hours of their time in interviews with us, but also provided extensive comments on previous iterations of the report. We also want to thank the interview respondents from these two states who are not identified in the report; their input was of much benefit to us.

RAND colleagues and project members Laura Zakaras and Jennifer Novak provided invaluable feedback throughout the project, and Catherine Augustine and Sue Bodilly offered additional comments and suggestions through RAND Education's Quality Assurance process. Jeri O'Donnell's careful editing greatly improved the text.

Finally, we would like to thank The Wallace Foundation for its continued support for building knowledge and research capacity in arts and cultural policy. Thanks especially to Ann Stone, Senior Research and Evaluation Officer, and Lee Mitgang, Director of Editorial Services, with whom we interacted regularly and happily over the course of this work.

While thanking the many individuals that contributed to this report, we retain sole responsibility for its contents.

CHAPTER ONE

Introduction

Most of America's state arts agencies (SAAs) were created to take advantage of federal arts funds that became available at the founding of the National Endowment for the Arts (NEA) in 1965 (Netzer, 1978; Larson, 1983; Mark, 1991).[1,2] The NEA's founders believed that state governments would be better able than a federal agency to find and nurture artists and arts organizations in small towns and rural areas; they also believed that public arts funding decisions should not be dominated by a centralized arts bureaucracy. As a result, they encouraged the states to set up SAAs (U.S. Congress, 1961; Scott, 1970; Larson, 1983). The federal pass-through to the states, however, was not automatic: To receive NEA money, states were required to form their own arts agencies and make financial commitments to them through legislative appropriations. The goal was to ensure a broad base of political support for public funding of the arts. State residents—and, more immediately, their elected representatives—had to like SAA programs enough to help pay for them.

SAAs have already helped to achieve two of the founders' main objectives: Professional artists and arts organizations can now be found in towns and rural areas as well as larger cities across America, and state and local agencies are now responsible for distributing the lion's share of public arts grants (Kreidler, 1996; McCarthy et al., 2001; Barsdate, 2003). Achieving broad-based political support, however, has proven problematic. Despite indications that the majority of Americans believe in government funding for the arts (Pettit and DiMaggio, 1997; DiMaggio and Pettit, 1999), SAAs and other governmental arts agencies in recent years have struggled to translate generic public goodwill into effective political support (Wyszomirski, 1995; Lowell, 2004).[3]

---

[1] This report focuses on the arts agencies of the 50 U.S. states. Except where indicated, the analysis does not include arts agencies for the six U.S. special jurisdictions: American Samoa, the District of Columbia, Guam, Puerto Rico, the Northern Mariana Islands, and the Virgin Islands.

[2] Six of the seven SAAs established prior to 1965 were voluntary organizations that received almost no state money. The New York State Council on the Arts was a notable exception. See Netzer, 1978.

[3] Wyszomirski (1995), for example, argues that "while the American public may indicate positive attitudes towards the arts, these are seldom translated into active participation in the arts or firm support for governmental arts agencies" (p. 25).

By the 1990s, some SAA leaders had decided that their long-standing approaches to building and retaining political support were no longer working (RAND interviews).[4] Tight state budgets and a movement to "reinvent government" had created economic and political challenges for all state government agencies, and SAAs were among the most vulnerable. Finding themselves under threat, SAA leaders began seeking new ways to convince state officials to put the arts—and their agencies—higher on the list of governmental priorities. It was not simply a question of bolstering budgets, although SAAs certainly faced a tighter funding environment. Rather, these leaders wanted to obtain a "place at the table" of state government; that is, they wanted to make the arts an integral part of governmental planning for the future of their states.

This report identifies strategic issues faced by SAA leaders as they seek to solidify political support and expand public funding for the arts and their agencies. It is the second in a series of reports describing the findings of a RAND Corporation study of the changing missions and roles of SAAs. The Wallace Foundation has been funding the study as part of the State Arts Partnerships for Cultural Participation (START) initiative it launched in 2001. Through START, Wallace gave 13 SAAs multiyear grants in support of innovative programs, research, and outreach efforts aimed at increasing arts participation in their states.[5] More broadly, the START initiative was intended to identify, collect, and disseminate strategies that promise to strengthen SAAs' ability to serve state residents.

Our examination of the historical relations between SAAs and state governments suggests that elected officials in most states have had little input into SAA decision-making. In large part this was because of the way that SAAs were envisioned—and structured—by their founders, who believed in distancing arts grantmaking from possible political influence (Cwi, 1983; Mulcahy, 2002). But there is tension between this original, "arm's-length" approach to state government and SAAs' ability to attract and retain political support. Our research suggests that in recognition of this, some SAAs have begun to align their missions and goals more closely with the policy agendas of state government officials. Their aim is to work with state officials to catalyze and nurture state cultural activity—without allowing their agencies to become politicized in the process.

---

[4] We define *SAA leaders* as the executive director and assistant or deputy director of an SAA, plus the members of the SAA's board.

[5] The 13 START states are Arizona, California, Connecticut, Kentucky, Massachusetts, Minnesota, Mississippi, Montana, New Jersey, North Carolina, Ohio, South Carolina, and Washington.

Research Approach

This study was informed by structured and informal interviews with current and past SAA staff and board members, NEA staff, and arts policy consultants and researchers.[6] Between April 2002 and November 2005, RAND researchers conducted over 100 in-person, telephone, and e-mail interviews and substantive conversations with individuals from 28 states. Those interviewed were staff and board members from 23 SAAs, as well as state legislators, arts advocates, and past and former SAA grantees from Maine and Montana. The interviews covered a range of issues designed to provide qualitative insights into SAAs' strategic thinking within the different state contexts. Topics included relations between staff and board, the nature of SAA advocacy efforts, methods for expanding the SAA constituency base, and SAA history.

Our discussions of SAA history and state government structure are supported by a comprehensive survey of the literature on SAAs and the NEA, plus a review of the relevant academic literature on public administration. Our thinking about the current and future direction of SAAs has been greatly influenced by attendance at statewide, regional, and national arts policy conferences and by participation in more than 15 START-related telephone conferences and workshops. Where possible, we support our conclusions with analyses of published and unpublished data generously provided by the National Assembly of State Arts Agencies (NASAA) and the NEA, as well as published data from the National Conference of State Legislatures (NCSL) and the National Association of State Budget Officers (NASBO).[7]

Because the study involved 50 separate organizations, our portrayal of the past experience and current behavior of SAAs is necessarily broad-brush. We recognize that SAAs vary widely with respect to, among other things, the size of their budgets, the character of their state arts communities, the strength of their state economies, and the attitudes of state residents toward government and governmental support of the arts.[8] Whereas some SAAs have a long history of strong board-based governance and close relations with elected officials, our findings suggest that more of them (especially in the West) fit the historical profile sketched out in this report. Nonetheless, all SAAs face trade-offs connected with arm's-length versus "arm-in-arm" approaches to state government, and it seems likely that SAAs (like many other government organizations) will be more effective if they are able to address the issues of legitimacy and support, operational capacity, and public value that are described in Chapter Six.

---

[6] Throughout this report, we use the terms *board* and *board members* to refer to, respectively, the governing or advisory body of an SAA and the members of that body.

[7] We have particularly benefited from access to data from NASAA's Profile Survey, a periodic survey of the leadership, structure and authority, partnerships, and grant distribution policies of all SAAs; and from access to NEA Partnership Agreement narratives for fiscal years 2001–2004.

[8] By *arts community*, we mean the artists and nonprofit arts organizations that are potential recipients of SAA grants, plus those who regularly consume the art these artists and organizations produce.

To deepen the understanding of issues associated with SAAs' efforts to integrate themselves more fully into state government, this report includes case studies of two SAAs—the Montana Arts Council and the Maine Arts Commission—that have taken bold and innovative steps in this regard. We obtained the information for these case studies through site visits to the agencies and telephone interviews with approximately 30 current and past SAA staff and board members, current and past SAA grantees, and state legislators, all of which took place between November 2003 and April 2005. We also reviewed a number of published and unpublished historical documents provided by the two agencies.

We chose the Montana agency as one of our cases because we had learned of it through the START initiative and were struck by agency leaders' willingness and ability to tackle a severe political problem head-on. We chose the Maine case because NASAA suggested it to us as an example of a successful effort to craft a mission that has engendered widespread public and political support. However, we recognize that these two agencies are not particularly representative (both are small and located in highly rural states, and certain aspects of their situations are, of course, unique) and that details of their strategies may not be applicable to other SAAs. Nevertheless, important elements of these two agencies' experiences are similar to those of other SAAs seeking to strengthen their position within state government. They thus help to clarify the rewards—and the risks—of bringing the arts and political worlds closer together.

Report Overview

Chapter Two of this report provides a brief overview of the structure of SAAs, describing how the arm's-length principle of governance operated in their early years (roughly 1965–1980), and how it has helped distance them from the political process in their states. Chapter Three analyzes the state-level political and budgetary trends over the last 20 years that are making the arm's-length principle untenable for SAAs in the future. Chapters Four and Five present, respectively, our case studies of the Montana Arts Council and the Maine Arts Commission, which illustrate SAAs' vulnerability to such trends and point to ways they might overcome it. Chapter Six considers the cases—and the situation of SAAs more generally—in light of a framework for public-sector management developed by Harvard University's Mark H. Moore, who emphasizes the need for strong agency leadership in choosing an appropriate mission and obtaining political support for it. Chapter Seven, the final chapter, concludes by summarizing the risks and rewards to SAAs of an arm-in-arm approach to state government.

CHAPTER TWO

At Arm's Length

At their founding, in the 1960s, SAAs' legislatively mandated purposes were predominantly broad in scope, allowing for a variety of possible activities. Adams (1966, p. 8) summarizes these mandated purposes as follows:[1]

> To stimulate and encourage presentations of performing arts and fine arts[;] to encourage public interest in the arts[;] to make surveys of public and private institutions engaged in artistic and cultural activities[;] to make recommendations on methods to encourage participation in, and appreciation of, the arts to meet the needs of the state[; and] to encourage freedom of artistic expression.

But although SAAs' mandated purposes were diverse, the means chosen to achieve them were not. Following the example of the NEA—and before it, the New York State Council on the Arts (NYSCA)—SAAs were set up to make grants to artists and arts organizations (Scott, 1970; Netzer, 1978).[2] Therefore, just as they had with NYSCA and the NEA, arts community leaders sought ways to ensure freedom of grantmaking choice for SAAs and freedom from political interference for SAA grantees. These leaders were convinced that direct government support for the arts would bring great benefits to state residents, but they also believed that the benefits could not be achieved if public arts funding was subjected to the vicissitudes of state politics.[3]

For their part, state elected leaders held differing views on whether to link government and the arts and, if so, how closely (Netzer, 1978; Mark, 1991; Mulcahy, 2002). Some were opposed to any direct government support of the arts at all. Others were primarily interested in securing the federal arts money that was promised in return for establishing an arts agency in their states. A few saw an opportunity to enrich the lives

---

[1] These purposes are also quoted in Mulcahy, 2002, p. 69.

[2] NYSCA was, in turn, modeled after the Arts Council of Great Britain, which was founded in 1946. The term *arm's length* was first used (in the context of the arts) to describe the governance structure of the Arts Council of Great Britain (Chartrand and McCaughey, 1989).

[3] In fact, some prominent artists and arts organizations—including, notably, the American Symphony Orchestra League—initially opposed the creation of the NEA because they feared it would lead to political interference in the arts. See, for example, U.S. Congress, 1961, 1962; Netzer, 1978; Mark, 1991; Zeigler, 1994.

of state residents and advance the national and international reputations of their states. But on one issue, all politicians agreed: No one wanted to be blamed for funding works that might insult or offend state residents. The politicians sought protection from the arts community just as the arts community sought protection from them (Chartrand and McCaughey, 1989; Cummings, 1991; Williams, 2003).

Despite stemming from different motivations, the shared desire of the arts community and elected officials to insulate the arts from politics had structural and organizational implications for the fledgling SAAs. First, like NYSCA (but not the NEA), SAAs were placed under the governance of unpaid citizen boards rather than within hierarchical organizational structures. Second, their decisionmaking processes were designed to incorporate the concerns of the arts community rather than those of elected officials. Together, these features of SAAs have protected state arts grantmaking from overt politicization. We argue, however, that they have also made it more difficult to get and retain the attention of elected officials.

SAA Governance Structure and Decisionmaking Processes

The board-based model of public-sector governance, in which an intermediary body is given overall responsibility for setting the policies and allocating the resources of a government agency, was adopted by all 50 SAAs at their founding (NCSL, 1981; Chartrand and McCaughey, 1989). For SAAs, the intermediary is a board whose members (15 on average) are appointed by government officials but serve without pay as private citizens.[4] In approximately three-quarters of the states, the governor appoints all SAA board members; in the remainder, legislators or the directors of departments in which SAAs are located appoint some of the members.

Most SAAs were established as independent government agencies, and despite many state government reorganizations over the years, three-quarters of them either are still fully independent or operate autonomously within umbrella departments.[5] Eight SAAs are embedded within larger departments that have final authority over their policies, their grantmaking decisions, or both; nominally, these agencies' boards

---

[4]   Five states legally require their SAAs to have legislators on their boards, although in two of these states they are not voting members. The Board of Trustees for the Vermont Arts Council has one gubernatorial appointee; the other board members are elected by the membership.

[5]   See NEA, 1978; Backas, 1980; NASAA, 1992a; 2000–2001 NASAA Profile Survey. By "operated autonomously," we mean their boards were responsible for developing and implementing policies and programs and for approving grants, with little or no reference to other executive branch agencies of state government. See Appendix A for more details on the position of SAAs within state governments.

are advisory rather than governing.[6] One SAA, the Vermont Arts Council, has never been part of state government at all. Instead, it is a private nonprofit membership organization that serves as the state-designated fiscal agent for public arts funds (NEA, 1978).

Elected officials (governors and legislators) determine the total amount of state money that SAAs receive; but for all but eight SAAs, it is the boards that are ultimately responsible for how the money is spent. Boards do not have complete discretion, as some state funds are earmarked for particular uses. For example, legislators in a number of states can direct funds to favored cultural projects and institutions through the use of supplementary line items not under SAA control. In many states, legislators also decide how much the agency may spend on its own administration versus programs. Nevertheless, boards are responsible for most decisions about development of new programs, discontinuation of programs, and allocations across programs, as well as for approving individual grants.

The boards of government agencies—together with their directors and, where relevant, the directors of the departments in which they sit—are accountable to state officials and the public for the appropriate, efficient, and wise use of taxpayer dollars. One aspect of this is financial: Boards must ensure that their agencies do not misuse or waste public funds. But political responsiveness is just as important: Boards are expected to develop programs and policies that are valued by state residents and, by extension, their elected representatives. Boards are also expected to keep political leaders mindful of the importance of the agency's mission and to inform them of the agency's achievements with respect to that mission. Thus, while SAA boards are generally discouraged from lobbying legislators on behalf of their agency's budget, they are not only allowed but expected to advocate for its mission.[7]

The policies and programs established by SAA boards are guided and administered by paid professional staffs and managed by an executive director. In 17 states, the director is appointed by the governor or hired by the head of the department in which the agency is embedded. In 27 states, the director is hired by the board or some subset of the board.[8] In six states, the director is hired by some combination of the board, the

---

[6] Respondents from two of these states told us that although their SAA boards technically serve in an advisory capacity only, they have retained much of their influence over policy and grantmaking. In one state, Iowa, the board is advisory to the executive director.

[7] Advocacy is not the same as lobbying. The Internal Revenue Service defines *lobbying* as a communication to legislators, or urging the public to communicate with legislators, in order to influence specific legislation. *Advocacy*, a broader term, means promoting a point of view on an issue (Center for Nonprofit Management, 2004). In this report, we define *SAA advocacy* as "making the case for public arts funding," using the term *lobbying* most often in the context of pushing for a specific increase (or resisting a proposed decrease) in a state's legislative appropriation for its SAA.

[8] These figures are based on data provided in NASAA, 1992a, as well as the authors' June 2005 review of state statutes.

governor, and the department head. In all states, those who hire or appoint the director are also responsible for dismissing him or her, even though, as Figure 2.1 illustrates, a politically appointed director must report both to the board and to the governor or department head. Even political appointees, however, are typically hired for their professional qualifications rather than patronage. Political ties between directors and governors are typically not very strong—if they exist at all.[9]

Finally, in addition to the assistance they receive from their staffs, SAA boards are aided by outside panels of arts professionals and lay experts who review grant applications and rank them according to artistic quality and other merits.[10] In no state do these panelists have formal authority to decide which grant applications to fund and to what amount, but SAA boards rarely overturn a panel recommendation.[11] Panelists, together with other members of the arts community, also help SAAs design their programs and determine their grant guidelines and evaluation criteria (NASAA, 1992b). This is done both informally and as part of periodic statewide strategic planning efforts. Through these mechanisms, members of the arts community exert significant influence on SAA policies, programs, and priorities.

Advantages of SAA Governance and Decisionmaking

The advantages that board-governed agencies have over agencies headed by a single executive include bringing greater numbers of ordinary people into public life, gathering together experts in a particular field to advise on specialized issues, and encouraging partnerships between government and private interests (Hogwood, 1995). Further, boards that are geographically, culturally, and occupationally diverse should, in principle, be better able than a single individual to represent the needs and interests of a wide range of citizens, thereby providing an important "reality check" on policymaking.[12] And because board members represent a number of legislative districts, are more apt to know legislators socially, and, as volunteers, are less constrained by state anti-lobbying

---

[9]   According to Wilson (1989), length of service is one indication of how strong an executive's political ties are. Our calculations based on NASAA data indicate that in 2003, one-third of the politically appointed SAA directors had held their jobs for ten years or more, which is much longer than the two years or less typical of political appointments. One of our reviewers commented that he knows of no SAA director that has been appointed based on his or her political connections.

[10]   Panelists are not paid a salary, but SAAs cover their travel expenses and, in some states, give them small honorariums. SAA board members frequently serve on panels and as panel chairs. In 1991, Maryland was the only state to mandate that legislators be placed on panels (NASAA, 1992a).

[11]   This statement is based on RAND interviews, as well as information from NASAA, 1992b; SAA Websites; and the 2000–2001 NASAA Profile Survey.

[12]   According to the 2000–2001 NASAA Profile Survey, approximately one-third of the states require their SAA boards to be geographically representative, and 8 percent require them to be ethnically or racially diverse. Another 14 percent require other forms of representation. For example, Tennessee requires at least one of its SAA board members to be over 60 years old, and Iowa and West Virginia require their boards to be balanced by gender. However, one reviewer told us he believes that these board diversity requirements are regularly ignored.

Figure 2.1
Model of Governance for SAAs with a Politically Appointed Director

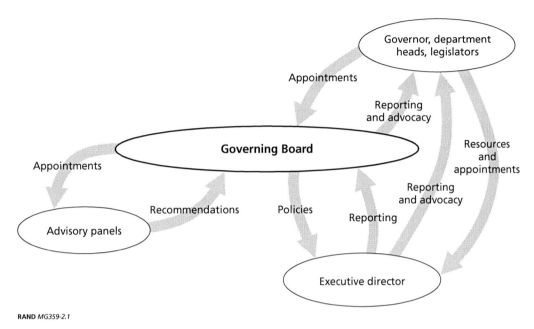

RAND *MG359-2.1*

laws, they may be better placed than a single director to inform and influence legislators and to gain insight into legislators' priorities.[13]

One of the greatest advantages of this arm's-length approach to governance is that, at least in theory, it eliminates some of the political pressures faced by government agencies created to distribute public money (Hogwood, 1995; Institute of Governmental Studies Library, 2005; California Governor's Office, 2005). For example, SAA boards are expected to resist pressure to give out more, or larger, grants to arts providers that are politically well connected or located in politically important legislative districts.[14] They are also expected to resist efforts by officials and others who would like them to give or deny grants on ideological grounds. Boards thus act as a buffer between politics and the arts, allowing non-partisan professional values and judgments to prevail over idiosyncratic political preferences.

---

[13] One of our reviewers said that, in fact, "SAA directors have many opportunities to educate elected officials, lobby behind the scenes, and establish surrogate lobbyists"—without putting themselves at risk of violating anti-lobbying laws.

[14] See, for example, Cwi, 1983; Chartrand and McCaughey, 1989; Devlin and Hoyle, 2000. According to Chartrand and McCaughey (p. 49), "Having been appointed by the government of the day, [board members] are expected to fulfill their grant-giving duties independent of the day-to-day interests of the party in power, much like the trustees of a blind trust."

This is not to say that board-governed agencies are immune to political pressure. But the following factors help them resist it:

- Board members are volunteers, so their careers and incomes do not depend on their board positions;
- Terms of service are generally staggered, so at least some board members are likely to have been appointed under a previous administration;
- Board members cannot easily be removed from their positions before their terms expire; and
- Decisionmaking is collective and typically takes place during open public meetings.

For SAAs, the fact that arts community constituents are substantially involved in decisionmaking also offers a number of advantages. Constituent involvement in strategic planning efforts helps SAAs assess constituent needs and thereby meet them more effectively. The use of panels to help determine grant eligibility and evaluation criteria and to recommend individual grants militates against possible political, ideological, or personal biases in grantmaking (Galligan, 1993; Mulcahy, 1995; RAND interviews).[15] To ensure that panelists are unbiased and professional, they are chosen for their expertise in specific art forms, their knowledge of local communities, and their arts management experience. When possible, they are also chosen for their geographic and cultural representativeness, although out-of-state panelists are used as necessary to avoid potential conflicts of interest. In the majority of states, panel meetings are open to the public, as are the board meetings in which applications are approved or denied and grant amounts decided.[16] Most SAAs also have rules in place that allow unsuccessful applicants to appeal in the event of a procedural irregularity.[17]

Disadvantages of SAA Governance and Decisionmaking

The primary disadvantage of board-governed agencies compared with agencies having hierarchical governance structures is that they tend to be less politically responsive and less visible to elected officials. One reason for this is that no single individual has the power or responsibility to decide agency policies or programs: Authority and political accountability are dispersed among agency leaders. In fact, the very traits that tend to

---

[15] Grant eligibility and evaluation criteria are clearly stated in SAA program guidelines. Some important eligibility criteria, such as nonprofit status, are mandated by state law.

[16] In 1991, 11 SAAs closed their panel meetings to the public, and four closed the board meetings at which they made grant decisions (NASAA, 1992a). A July 2005 review of SAA Websites indicates that several of these SAAs have since opened their meetings to the public.

[17] For example, an appeal might result if incorrect evaluation criteria were used, a panelist or SAA staff member had a conflict of interest, or information required of and submitted by an applicant was withheld. See Indiana Arts Commission, 2004b.

protect board-governed agencies from the illegitimate demands of elected officials also make them slower to respond to the legitimate demands (Little Hoover Commission, 1989; Hogwood, 1995; California Governor's Office, 2005).

A second and related disadvantage of board-governed agencies derives from the part-time, volunteer nature of their boards. According to Carver (1990), there is a tendency for all boards, including those in the private sector, to focus disproportionately on details rather than policy. Cwi (1983), who found this to be true for SAAs, suggested that it was in part because board members' time was dominated by the sheer volume of grantmaking. But Cwi also noted that SAA board members often "come to the council unfamiliar with its operations and programs, and find themselves inundated with grantmaking and policy decisions for which they are unprepared" (p. 43). More recently, in a survey of 14 SAAs, the Western States Arts Federation (WESTAF) found that some SAAs have board members who frequently fail to attend scheduled board meetings (WESTAF, 2000).[18] Boards whose members are unprepared for the job or that have difficulty obtaining a quorum to conduct business are not likely to provide their agencies with much leadership.

Efforts to introduce professional standards into grantmaking, and the panel review system in general, have also had political drawbacks for SAAs. For example, competitive grant programs that emphasize artistic quality and innovation—but do not take applicants' geographic location into account—can be politically problematic, because the grants awarded under such programs tend to be concentrated in urban areas. Accordingly, they hold little appeal for legislators from rural districts, who tend not to support SAAs during state budget negotiations.[19]

More profoundly, extensive arts community participation in SAA policies and programs has disadvantaged SAAs to the extent that it has encouraged the arts community—and current and former grantees, in particular—to view SAAs as "their" agencies. In the past, SAA leaders did not often challenge this view, believing that by meeting the needs of their arts constituents they would also meet the needs of the broader public. They expected state support for local artists and arts organizations to encourage a wide variety of state residents to increase their participation in and enjoyment of the arts. Widespread arts participation would in turn translate into widespread political support for SAAs (Lowell, 2004).

This, however, has not happened—or, at least, not to the extent that SAA leaders had hoped. One reason may be that while artists and arts organizations are direct beneficiaries of SAA grants, the extent of the benefits provided by these grants to the

---

[18] The SAAs surveyed were those of Arizona, Colorado, Indiana, Kentucky, Minnesota, Missouri, Montana, New Mexico, Nevada, New York, Oregon, Pennsylvania, Texas, and Virginia. According to WESTAF (2000, p. 9), "Unlike private nonprofit organizations, SAAs can introduce but not enforce mechanisms that facilitate the removal of non-attending board members."

[19] See, for example, Hernandez, 2003; Sabulis, 2004. This point was made by several respondents.

majority of Americans is difficult to assess. Certainly, only a fraction of Americans regularly pass through the doors of the nonprofit arts organizations that receive the biggest chunk of state arts funding (Lowell, 2004). These arts attenders are on average older and better educated than other Americans.[20] They are also significantly more likely to be white, to be female, and to reside in urban areas (Nichols, 2003). When state budgets are flush, this is not necessarily a problem: Arguments can be made for public support of many small but worthy groups. Given current political and budgetary trends, however, SAAs must be able to demonstrate that they serve a wide spectrum of state residents and that those residents highly value the arts experiences that SAAs make possible.

Advocacy

In the early years, much of the SAA and state arts community advocacy focused on acquiring funds for and from the NEA rather than from state legislatures (Netzer, 1978).[21] According to one of our reviewers, in her state this was not because advocates viewed state officials as particularly hostile to the arts. It was, rather, simply a matter of everyone concerned understanding that the NEA would be the agency's primary source of funding.[22] Since about the mid-1980s, however, most if not all SAAs have focused their efforts on building political support at home. We have identified four main strategies that SAA leaders have pursued over time:

- Encourage politically powerful grantees to lobby for the SAA;
- Cultivate one or more "arts champions" within the legislature;
- Meet with elected officials; and
- Create statewide citizens' advocacy groups.

The first of these strategies is to encourage politically powerful grantees, which are often but not always major arts organizations, to lobby for increases to the agency's budget. In return, these grantees expect to continue receiving grants from the agency

---

[20] As defined by the NEA's Survey on Public Participation in the Arts, arts attenders are those that attend the "benchmark" arts activities: jazz, classical music, opera, musicals, plays, ballets, and art museums. According to the 2002 Survey on Public Participation in the Arts, almost 40 percent of American adults participated in a benchmark arts activity at least once in 2002 (Nichols, 2003). However, since 1982, rates of attendance at live cultural events, with the exception of art museums and jazz concerts, have significantly declined. The pattern has been observed among almost all age, gender, and education groups (DiMaggio and Mukhtar, 2004).

[21] This was not universally true, as evidenced by a comment made by one of our respondents: "We don't think SAAs at any time in our history worked harder for the NEA budget than we did for our own budgets."

[22] The NEA, too, expected SAAs to devote their time to advocating for its budget in return for the federal block grants they received. In fact, as reported by Weaver (1988), Nancy Hanks, Chairman of the NEA from 1970 to 1970, encouraged the creation of NASAA primarily to strengthen state-level advocacy for the NEA.

(Arian, 1989; Savage, 1989). The second strategy is to cultivate arts champions; that is, persons within the legislature who will look out for the SAA during state budget negotiations (Barsdate, 2001; McBride, 2005). The third strategy is for SAA leaders to get to know state officials personally in order to inform them about SAA programs and activities and convince them of their value (NASAA, 2003b). Finally, the fourth strategy is to encourage the formation of statewide citizens' advocacy groups able to "organize the arts constituencies in their states, educate the public on the importance of art to the life of the community, publicize the need for greater state support, represent the interests of artists, and, most importantly, put pressure on legislatures to adequately support the state arts council" (Dworkin, 1991, p. 200).

While all of these strategies have at times been useful, they have not succeeded in convincing most state officials that public support for SAAs is consistent or widespread. Quid pro quo arrangements with major arts organizations, for example, are problematic because despite efforts to diversify their audiences, these organizations still serve a relatively narrow segment of the state population (Nichols, 2003). Further, in a number of states, the major arts organizations will no longer lobby for the SAAs because SAA grants represent such a small proportion of their revenues (RAND interviews). Arts-champion strategies are risky because they can create the impression that SAAs and their grantees are the pet projects of individual legislators or political parties, rather than bipartisan organizations delivering value to the state as a whole (Guinane, 2005).[23] They have also left SAAs vulnerable to legislative turnover—a problem exacerbated in recent years by the introduction of term limits in 15 states (NCSL, 2005b).[24]

According to the experts, the "getting to know you" strategy is fundamental to successful advocacy (Avner, 2002; NASAA, 2003b). In theory, SAA board members should be well placed to make such contacts; McBride (2005), for example, suggests that board members "can be the most powerful arts advocates in their states" (p. 43).[25] But this strategy requires regular contacts with legislators throughout the year, not simply quick introductions in the midst of state budget negotiations. Board members therefore must have a high level of commitment to the agency and a fairly deep understanding of its programs and goals, which, as mentioned above, has not always been

---

[23] The formation of a legislative arts caucus prevents an SAA from appearing to be the pet project of an individual legislator but does not necessarily avoid the appearance of partisanship. See, for instance, Yee, 2001.

[24] For example, in Maine we were told of a legislator who became Speaker of the House in the 1970s. He supported the arts and the arts agency in that capacity for 20 years—until term limits forced him to retire. His retirement coincided with sharp cuts to the Maine Arts Commission's legislative appropriation. According to our respondents, the Commission might still have suffered the cuts had the legislator remained in office—but its cause was not helped by his absence.

[25] Board members sometimes are (or feel themselves to be) constrained "to follow the vision of the governor," and are therefore unable or unwilling to push to expand SAA budgets beyond what the governor has requested (McBride, 2005, p. 44). But the getting-to-know-you strategy does not require lobbying per se. Rather, it is a long-term approach designed to build legislators' awareness and understanding of the agency's goals and its progress toward those goals.

the case. In years past, at any rate, SAA board members tended to spend little time positioning their agencies for success in future budget negotiations (Arey, 1975; Cwi, 1983; RAND interviews). As a result, in many states responsibility for advocacy has devolved on SAA directors, who are already handicapped by anti-lobbying laws.[26]

The most promising advocacy strategy for SAAs may be the formation of broad-based citizen advocacy groups. Ideally, such groups are highly diverse in terms of members' artistic interests, political affiliations, and legislative districts. They can therefore legitimately claim to represent a wide variety of state residents who support state funding of the arts. The main drawback to this strategy is that the funding priorities of such groups do not always coincide with those of SAAs.[27] Moreover, their heavy dependence on volunteers may cause their efforts to be inconsistent. While achieving notable successes at "crisis lobbying," they often fail to maintain the long-term advocacy needed to avoid such crises in the first place (Dworkin, 1991; McBride, 2005).[28]

Insulation and Isolation

A problem common to all the strategies examined is that they have been carried out in an ad hoc and inconsistent way. Faced with the need to stretch very small budgets, SAAs have in the past typically been opportunistic rather than systematic in their approaches to building political support (RAND interviews).

A deeper problem, however, derives from SAAs' own arm's-length governance structure and decisionmaking processes. These features of SAAs have been quite successful at insulating state arts grantmaking from political interference. SAA staff and board members design their own programs and choose which artists and arts organizations to support, accepting significant input from the arts community and very little from elected officials. Professional assessments of artistic quality are weighted heavily in most grantmaking decisions, whereas considerations such as local employment are not. SAAs must, of course, abide by state anti-obscenity and anti-pornography laws, and some SAAs try to avoid funding works of art that seem likely to be highly controversial (Free Expression Policy Project, 2003). In a few states, legislators have mandated

---

[26] One reviewer commented that SAA board members are often unable to advocate effectively for the agency—or to provide strong leadership—because distrustful directors and staff actively work to disempower them. In his view, SAAs' complex grantmaking process "keeps the SAA director in control and assures that the board members are kept at bay."

[27] For example, in a 2002 survey funded by WESTAF, SAA directors expressed concerns "about the degree to which agencies and advocacy groups actually share common goals. In some states, this issue was said to be exacerbated by conflicts described as 'center versus periphery' or 'north versus south,' related to the geographic concentration of arts organizations in some areas of a state" (Betty, 2002, p. 4).

[28] We are not suggesting that SAAs can always avoid budget cuts. Events such as state fiscal crises affect all state agencies and are entirely out of their control. However, sustained and strategic advocacy should help SAAs avoid situations in which their very existence is threatened.

a degree of geographic equity in the distribution of SAA grants.[29] But the top-down governmental control over the arts that was feared by early opponents of public arts funding has not materialized.

However, the considerable managerial discretion of SAA leaders may have come at a price, isolating SAAs and undermining their relevance to policymaking at the state level. Many state legislators appear not to understand exactly what SAAs do; others view SAA programs as valuable but not essential to most of their constituents' lives (RAND interviews). As one former SAA leader put it, state legislators, and the public, tend to see state-level support for the arts as a "nice-to-have" but not a "have-to-have"—in other words, a luxury to be dispensed with when state budgets are tight.

---

[29] According to NASAA (1992a), decentralized grantmaking is mandated by law in Massachusetts, New York, and North Carolina. Many more states have voluntarily adopted decentralization programs.

CHAPTER THREE

Catalysts for Change

In the 2000s, SAAs face a different and in some ways more difficult economic and political environment than they did in their early years. State appropriations for SAAs now far outpace SAA funding from the NEA, reducing SAAs' dependence on the NEA but increasing their vulnerability to highly volatile state budgets.[1] In fact, state expenditures on the arts since 1989 have lost ground compared to other types of state expenditures, and prospects for the growth of state general funds, the predominant financing source for SAAs, are discouraging. SAAs must also cope with a pronounced shift in American attitudes toward the roles and responsibilities of government. Voters today demand greater responsiveness and accountability from government than they once did (Osborne and Gaebler, 1992; Kettl, 1998). As suggested in the previous chapter, governmental activities deemed "nonessential" are susceptible to elimination. Accordingly, some SAAs believe that their low visibility with the politicians who authorize their budgets—and with the residents of their states—has become a liability. In this chapter, we outline the trends that are acting as catalysts for change in a number of SAAs, including our two case study agencies in Montana and Maine.

Budgetary Trends

When SAAs were first established, legislators in many states were not convinced of the value of SAA programs to state residents—or, at any rate, they were happy to let the federal government pay for them (Scott, 1971; Netzer, 1978; Mark, 1991). Not until 1974, eight years after grants to SAAs first became available through the NEA's Federal-State Partnership program, did all 50 state legislatures choose to appropriate state money for an SAA (NASAA, 2000a).[2] As Figure 3.1 shows, in that year 20 states appropriated less than $100,000 each for their SAA, and just seven appropriated

---

[1] Historically, state revenues and expenditures have had a higher variance than federal revenues and expenditures (NASBO, 1995).

[2] For comparability to NEA and state expenditure data, the legislative appropriations cited in this report include line items unless otherwise specified. Note, however, that legislative appropriation data are not perfectly

Figure 3.1
Distribution of SAA Legislative Appropriations Across States, 1974

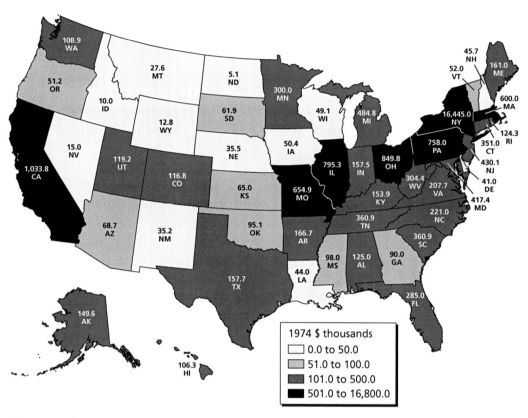

SOURCE: Authors' calculations based on data from NEA, 1978.
RAND *MG359-3.1*

more than $500,000. The median appropriation was $124,000, or five cents per capita (NEA, 1978). The variance in state-level funding across states was (and still is) high. For example, the most generous state, New York, appropriated $16.4 million, or 91 cents per capita; the least generous state, North Dakota, appropriated just $5,100, or one cent per capita.

By the mid-1980s, however, the states had collectively caught up to the federal government in contributions to public arts dollars. As Figure 3.2 illustrates, almost 70 percent of SAAs in 1974 received less than half of their public revenues from their state legislatures, whereas just over 30 percent received half or more. By 1984, these

---

comparable across states. For example, in the legislative appropriation figures reported to NASAA, some states include program funds raised through "percent for art" mechanisms (such as funds for public art projects raised through taxes on construction of new state buildings), whereas other states do not.

Figure 3.2
SAA Public Funding Represented by State Legislative Appropriations, Selected Years

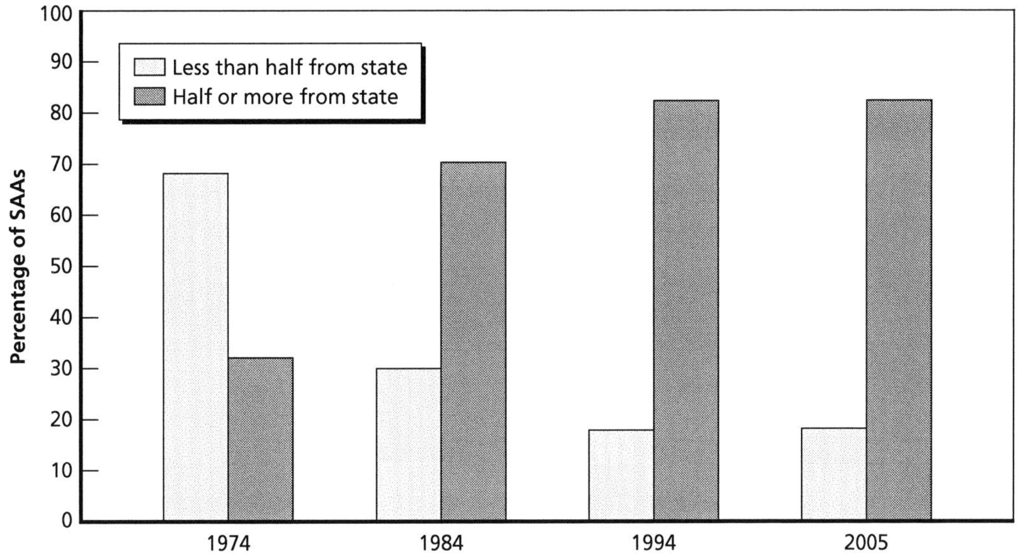

SOURCE: Authors' calculations based on data from NASAA and from NEA Annual Reports, various years.
RAND *MG359-3.2*

shares had been reversed.[3] By 1994, most SAAs' legislative appropriations had far out-stripped what they received from the NEA, with the median legislative appropriation reaching $2.0 million and the median federal amount just $695,000. By 2005, the median legislative appropriation was $2.5 million and the median federal amount was $616,000.

Figure 3.3 reveals that this turnabout took place for two reasons: because of increases in state legislative appropriations for SAAs and because of declines in the federal legislative appropriation for the NEA. The inflation-adjusted NEA budget grew quite rapidly in the 1970s, with proportionate growth in federal arts grants to the states.[4] But beginning in 1980, the federal appropriation for the NEA began to decline. Since 1985, total state appropriations for the 50 SAAs have exceeded the federal appropriation for the NEA in every year (NASAA, 2000a; NEA, 1985). If NEA budget growth continues to be flat or rises only modestly, as many observers believe it will,

---

[3]   As calculated here, "public revenue" for each SAA is the sum of its state legislative appropriation and its total NEA grants. For most SAAs, this measure of public revenue represents by far the bulk of total revenue; in 2005, for example, public revenue represented almost 90 percent of total SAA revenues (NASAA, 2005). Few SAAs receive much private funding; in 2005, only about 2 percent of total SAA revenues came from the private sector (NASAA, 2005).

[4]   Federal arts grants to the states have grown faster than NEA budgets over time because the pass-through rate has increased, from 20 percent in 1973 to 40 percent in 1996. However, the most recent increase in the pass-through rate, in 1996, was more than offset by cuts to the NEA budget (Lowell, 2004).

Figure 3.3
Inflation-Adjusted Federal and State Legislative Appropriations for SAAs and the NEA,
1974–2005

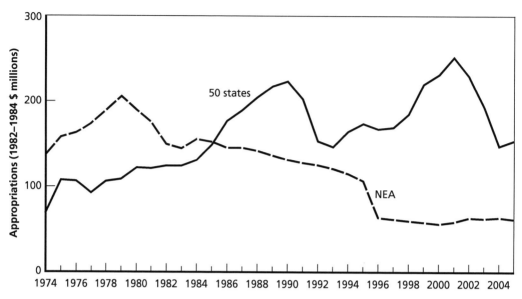

SOURCE: Authors' calculations based on NASAA and NEA data.
RAND *MG359-3.3*

state legislatures will likely continue to provide the bulk of SAA funding for the fore-seeable future (Hoekstra, 1997; Holman, 2000; Larson, 1997; Armbrust, 2004). And this is despite the recent sharp declines in state spending.

But just how rosy are SAAs' prospects for increases in state-level funding? State expenditure trends suggest that prospects for growth are unpromising at the state level as well. Figure 3.4 shows that between 1979 and 1989, state legislative appropriations for SAAs grew strongly, by 7 percent per year on average, which is in contrast to just under 3 percent for other state government activities financed out of state general funds.[5] This growth began from a very low base, however, and has not been sustained. In the early 1990s and again in the 2000s, SAAs across the country experienced cuts in their legislative appropriations. Overall, since 1989, state spending on the arts has not kept pace with other types of state general fund expenditures.

---

[5]   These figures are adjusted for inflation. The National Association of State Budget Officers (NASBO) (2006) defines general funds as the predominant source for financing a state's ongoing operations. General fund revenues derive from broad-based state taxes and are typically unrestricted in use. Data on general fund expenditures prior to 1979 are not available.

Figure 3.4
Inflation-Adjusted Growth of SAA Legislative Appropriations, State General Fund Expenditures, and Other State Expenditures, 1979–2005

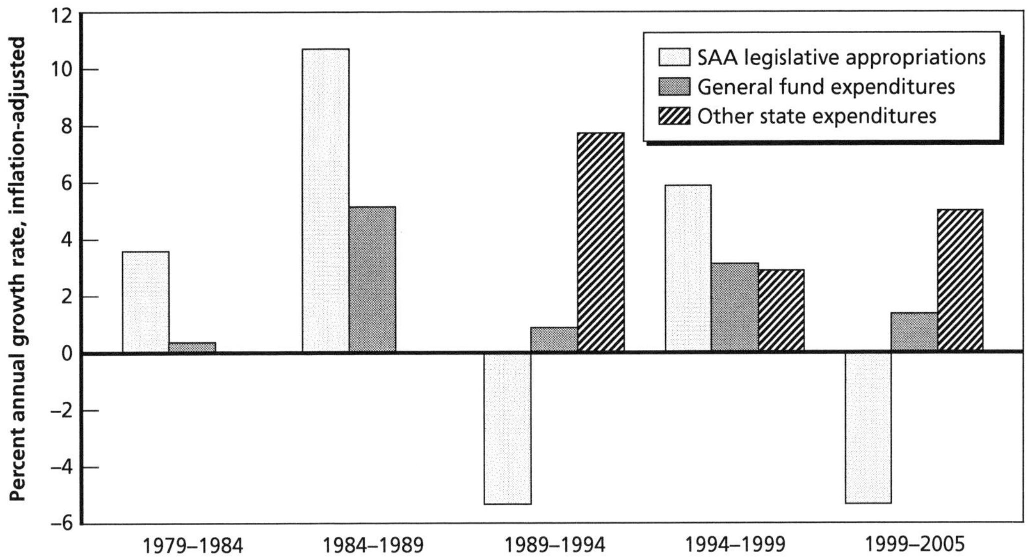

SOURCE: Authors' calculations based on data from NASAA, NASBO, and U.S. Census Bureau, various years.
RAND *MG359-3.4*

Further, state general funds are themselves under increasing pressure. On the expenditure side, the reasons include rapid growth in entitlement programs, such as Medicaid, and increasing numbers of unfunded federal mandates, such as the No Child Left Behind Act, Individuals with Disabilities Education Act, and various new measures introduced by the Department of Homeland Security.[6] On the revenue side, voter resistance to tax increases has been growing, leading state governments to increasingly rely on dedicated revenue streams to fund programs.[7] Thus, while general fund expenditures grew by just under 2 percent per year from 1989 to 2005, other types of state expenditures grew by over 5 percent (see Figure 3.4).[8] If this trend continues,

---

[6]   Unfunded federal mandates require state governments to provide services or goods without federal compensation. See Garrett and Wagner, 2004; NCSL, 2004; and General Accounting Office, 2004.

[7]   For example, four states (Florida, Massachusetts, Michigan, Missouri) have passed tax limits, two (Colorado, Oregon) have passed tax and spending limits, and 16 have adopted supermajority requirements for passing tax increases (NCSL, 2005a).

[8]   The "other state expenditures" category consists of total state expenditures less general fund expenditures; that is, expenditures out of revenue sources restricted by law for particular governmental functions or activities ("other state funds"), plus bond funds (NASBO, 2006). Data on other state expenditures for 1979–1989 were not available at the time of writing.

general funds will represent a declining share of the state revenue pie, which means that even if SAAs manage to maintain their share of general fund revenues, they will lose budgetary ground relative to other state government organizations.[9]

Finally, a basic fact of SAA life is that state legislatures have never made an abundance of public resources available for the arts. Despite their rapid growth early on, legislative appropriations for SAAs remain tiny relative to overall state budgets. Between 1979 and 2005, for example, only a handful of states devoted more than one-tenth of one percent (0.1 percent) of their general fund expenditures to their SAAs; in 2005, the average and median percentage across all states was just 0.05. As Figure 3.5 shows, 15 states devoted less than one-third of one percent of their state general fund expenditures to their SAAs in 2005. In comparison, 2004 spending on elementary and secondary education represented 35.7 percent of state general fund expenditures; Medicaid represented 16.9 percent; higher education, 11.9 percent; corrections, 7.0 percent; public assistance, 2.3 percent; and transportation, 0.6 percent (NASBO, 2006).[10]

Political Developments

Of course, the size of an agency's budget does not necessarily reflect its value to state residents. For example, most states still spend less on corrections than on higher education, but that does not mean their residents value state corrections departments less highly than state university systems. SAAs are valued by most members of the public who are aware of what they do (University of South Carolina, 2000; California Arts Council, 2001). It appears, however, that most Americans are not aware of what SAAs do: Surveys and opinion polls conducted in the 1990s and early 2000s suggest that many people do not even know their state has an arts agency (Ohio Arts Council, 2001; Hessenius, 2003; Lowell, 2004).

Low visibility for a government agency is not always a drawback, of course, especially when there is a chance of scandal or controversy. As noted in the previous chapter, SAAs' arm's-length governance structure was motivated in part by politicians wanting to distance themselves from potentially controversial arts grants. In fact, some states' legislators have been concerned enough about arts-related controversies to impose legal

---

[9]   Between 1989 and 2005, for instance, state funds dedicated to particular activities (e.g., gasoline taxes used to finance transportation projects) grew more than twice as fast as general funds (NASBO, 1990, 2006).

[10]   Figures for 2005 were not available, and the figure shown for corrections includes expenditures from the sale of bonds to build prisons.

Figure 3.5
Share of SAA Legislative Appropriations in State General Fund Expenditures, 2005

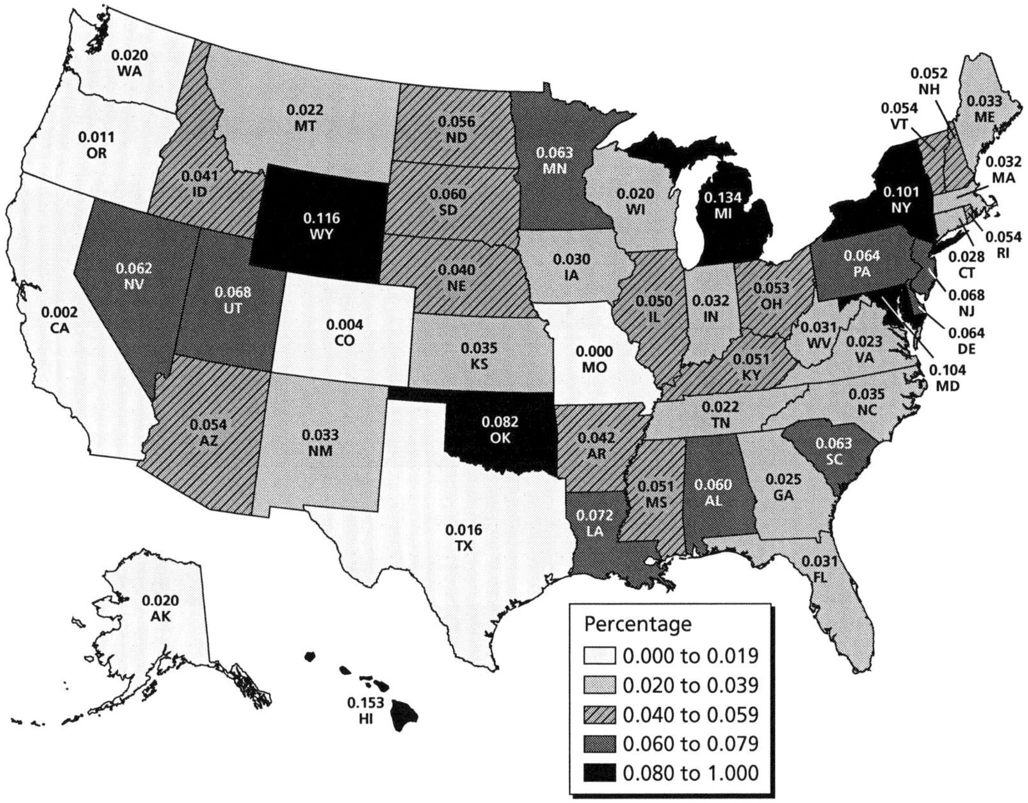

SOURCE: Authors' calculations based on data from NASBO and NASAA.
NOTES: SAA legislative appropriations, net line items; state general fund expenditures, net capital expenditures.
RAND *MG359-3.5*

restrictions on aspects of SAA grantmaking.[11] Some SAAs have therefore consciously chosen to maintain a low profile with legislators and the public, subscribing to the philosophy that too much attention could be dangerous (RAND interviews).[12]

---

[11] For example, the Texas legislature has added language to the legislation governing the Texas Commission on the Arts that is designed to inhibit it from funding art with sexual content (Free Expression Policy Project, 2003).

[12] In a study of the state of Washington's cultural agencies, for example, it was suggested that some of them may prefer to maintain a low public profile because they believe "most citizens would not want to support the arts or culture if they found out they were actually doing so" (Schuster, 2001, p. 34). By way of contrast, a public opinion poll commissioned by the Ohio Arts Council found that three-quarters of Ohioans favor using tax dollars to support the arts, but only 40 percent are aware that tax dollars are already used this way (Ohio Arts Council, 2001).

For most of their history, a low-profile strategy seems to have worked fairly well for SAAs. But in the current American political environment, government organizations across the board are finding it necessary to raise their visibility with politicians and the public. One reason for this change is that there are now many more groups and causes competing for government resources, and they are using increasingly sophisticated lobbying techniques (Petracca, 1992; Thurber, 1998). "Quiet" agencies risk being ignored in this highly competitive environment. Further, taxpayer demands for government that is more efficient and more effective (or for simply less government, period) have prompted officials to scrutinize agencies from the large to the small to determine whether their functions could be better performed by the private sector (Hedge, 1998; Peters, 2001). A number of state agencies—including some SAAs—have been asked not only to justify particular programs and activities, but also to defend their very existence.

While no SAAs have yet been eliminated, in several states they have come very close.[13] It is therefore essential for SAAs to trumpet their accomplishments if they are to convince elected leaders and the public that their activities in support of the arts are an appropriate, effective, and even indispensable use of state taxpayers' money (Minicucci, 2003; Moore and Moore, 2005). Given their extremely limited resources, they must also be strategic in the way they go about doing this.

The two chapters that follow present case studies of two SAAs, the Montana Arts Council and the Maine Arts Commission, that illustrate strategic approaches to managing the SAA political environment. The Montana case involves a crisis that was political in origin; the Maine case involves a crisis that was primarily economic.[14] In both cases, agency leaders acted quickly and decisively—in Montana, to save their agency from elimination; in Maine, to save their agency from irrelevancy. These agency leaders managed to strengthen relations with elected officials by demonstrating that agency programs and activities contribute to important public policy agendas and are highly valued by a large number of state residents.

---

[13] For example, several of our respondents commented that it was only the prospective loss of federal matching funds from the NEA that kept state legislators in California and Colorado from eliminating their SAAs altogether in 2003.

[14] Of course, it can be argued that cutbacks to agency budgets have a large political component regardless of the severity of the fiscal squeeze.

CHAPTER FOUR

Making the Case for the Arts in Montana

When the Montana State Legislature established the Montana Arts Council in 1967, it did so in recognition

> of the increasing importance of the arts in the lives of the citizens of Montana, of the need to provide opportunity for our young people to participate in the arts and to contribute to the great cultural heritage of our state and nation, and of the growing significance of the arts as an element which makes living and vacationing in Montana desirable to the people of other states. (Montana State Legislature, 2005)

Historically, the Council has always been one of the smallest SAAs, with never more than 11 full-time-equivalent staff. In fiscal year (FY) 2004, the Council's legislative appropriation out of the state's general fund was approximately $287,000, which was among the lowest for SAAs in absolute terms. Even per capita (Montana is a big, rural state), the legislative appropriation put the Council at 47th of 56 SAAs (NASAA, 2003a).

However, as can be seen in Figure 4.1, appropriations from the general fund are not the Council's only source of revenue. In FY 2004, they accounted for 17 percent of total revenues, while NEA grants accounted for 36 percent; a grant from The Wallace Foundation, 7 percent; and a public arts program funded by a tax on state construction projects, roughly 5 percent. Technically, one of the Council's single biggest sources of revenue was the Montana Cultural Trust, an endowment established in 1975 that is financed by a statewide tax on coal. In FY 2004, interest revenue from the Cultural Trust contributed about 35 percent to the Council's total revenues, with roughly 80 percent of it dedicated to grants in the arts.[1] It is not the Council, however, but the Montana legislature that determines the final recipients and amounts of all Cultural

---

[1]   The Cultural Trust revenue reported here includes supplemental funds from the state general fund. The Cultural Trust's function is to fund grants to organizations and projects sponsored by the Montana Historical Society, the State Historic Preservation Office, the Montana State Library, and the Montana Committee for the Humanities, as well as the Council, but all of these grants are passed through the Council's budget.

Figure 4.1
Revenue Sources for Montana Arts Council, FY 2004

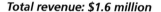

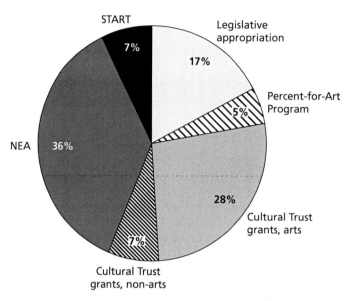

Total revenue: $1.6 million

SOURCE: Authors' calculations based on data provided by NASAA
and the Montana Arts Council.
RAND *MG359-4.1*

Trust grants (Montana Arts Council, 2004). According to reports from Council leaders, Council staff administer the Cultural Trust program but have limited influence over the choices made.[2]

Brief History of the Montana Arts Council

According to our respondents, for most of its history the Council functioned largely as it was set up to—as an independent agency operating on the margins of state government. Indeed, from 1967 until 1985, the Council was based in Missoula rather than the state capital, Helena. As of the mid-1990s, its 15 board members (all gubernatorial appointees) were quite active politically, but not particularly so with respect to the arts. The executive director, who is hired by the board, also did not consider advocacy to be an ongoing priority for the agency. Grantmaking to artists and arts organizations was the Council's primary activity, and grants were distributed widely across the state.

---

[2]   This point is disputed. One of our reviewers commented that the Council actually has a great deal of influence over Cultural Trust grant allocations.

Grantmaking decisions, with the exception of those for Cultural Trust grants, were largely insulated from the political realm.

Until the 1990s, contacts between the Council and elected officials were limited, consisting of occasional meetings with officials in the Governor's Office and a handful of longtime arts champions in the legislature. Advocacy at the state level was episodic because there was no sense of urgency about public funding for the arts. The citizens' arts advocacy group was dormant.[3] According to one respondent, some legislators perceived Council leaders to be elitist when it came to political dealing, behaving "as if they were above silly politics." At worst, Council staff "viewed the legislature as the enemy" (RAND interview). However, our respondents agree that for the most part, the Council ignored the legislature and the legislature ignored the Council.

A host of changes beginning in the early to mid-1990s dramatically affected the Council's political environment, catching it by surprise. Among the most significant were a shift to a significantly more conservative state legislature and the loss of several long-time arts champions from leadership positions within the legislature (Larmer et al., 1994; Yeoman, 1995). In addition, new budget-tightening measures meant that legislators usually sympathetic to the Council were divided by debates pitting one set of government-funded programs (primarily human services programs) against others, such as the arts.

Inspired in part by U.S. congressional attempts to eliminate the NEA, in 1997 a Montana state congressman authored legislation designed to eliminate the Council. Although his arguments for elimination emphasized fiscal conservatism, his attempt was supported by a significant number of legislators and state residents who not only believed that support of the arts was an inappropriate function of state government, but also had strong negative views of artists and the arts ("Block Attack on Arts," 1999; Hurdle, 2000).

Coincidentally, the Council was also undercut as the result of a campaign being conducted at the time by the Montana Historical Society. Historic buildings in the former territorial capital had recently come up for sale, and members of the Historical Society (with help from the National Trust for Historic Preservation) initiated a campaign to purchase them for the state (National Trust for Historic Preservation, 2003). However, because the primary source of public funding for historic preservation in Montana, the Cultural Trust, is also a major source of funding for the arts, another battle ensued. According to respondents, members and supporters of the Historical Society, who might have been the Council's natural allies in its fight for survival, instead became rivals over how to use Cultural Trust funds.

---

[3] Respondents reported that Montana has had a very small citizens' arts advocacy group since 1981, and that it followed the Council from Missoula to Helena in 1989. This advocacy group supports a part-time paid lobbyist for the arts at the state capitol.

All respondents agree that the Council's director, its board members, and a great many arts organizations and artists responded quickly and strongly to the crisis. In a grassroots advocacy effort, they contacted people throughout the state, mobilizing them to flood legislators' offices with phone calls and faxes in support of the agency.[4] This effort was successful in that opponents lost the battle to eliminate the Council, but half of the corpus of the Cultural Trust was given to the Historical Society, resulting in a significant cutback to Council staff, as well as to Cultural Trust grantmaking funds (Warshawski, 1999; RAND interviews).[5]

Montana's New Strategy: Marketing the Arts and the Agency

According to Council leaders, in the aftermath of the 1997 crisis they came to several realizations. First, they recognized that the Council was far more vulnerable politically than they had suspected. This vulnerability resulted in part from the political shift in the legislature, but it was also caused by the Council's deepening isolation. Council leaders had not had much success countering popular perceptions about the arts as activities for and by "long-haired, pot-smoking hippies" on the one hand and "elitists" on the other (RAND interview). Tellingly, many Montanans seemed unaware that the arts activities supported by the Council were the same as or similar to the arts activities that regularly engaged them and their families.[6]

Council leaders also realized that while an outcry from the arts community and a concerted effort by Council staff and board members had prevented the agency's elimination, they needed to build a broader base of support for its work. This meant broadening their conception of their constituency from the arts community to all citizens of Montana. Finally, the 1997 experience showed the Council that such allies as they had within government were neither sufficiently numerous nor sufficiently powerful. To avoid a repeat of the crisis, they needed to form new alliances and build new relationships with political leaders who could help put the agency on a firmer footing within state government.

In practical terms, Council leaders responded to their new circumstances by making an effort to generate more positive recognition for both the arts and the agency among state policymakers and the public (RAND interviews). Steps they took to achieve this included

---

[4] Council staff did not make phone calls themselves, as this would have violated Montana's anti-lobbying laws.

[5] The Cultural Trust corpus was loaned to the Historical Society with the expectation that it would eventually be restored through a general fund appropriation.

[6] See, for example, Montana Arts Council, 2005, for a description of some of the Council-supported and non-Council supported arts activities of Montanans.

- Emphasizing the ways in which Council programs benefit all state residents, rather than just artists and arts organizations;
- Changing the board's composition to include members with personal connections to Council opponents;[7]
- Appointing legislators opposed to public arts funding to panels in an effort to incorporate them into the Council's work; and
- Reaching out to opponents with personal calls, meetings, and invitations to visit the Council.

Nevertheless, Council leaders were still uncomfortable with the idea of elevating long-term relations with elected officials to a managerial and organizational priority.

In 2001, the Council was chosen as one of 13 SAA grantees in The Wallace Foundation's multiyear START initiative. According to Council leaders, the timing was perfect. Exposure to public management concepts introduced by Mark H. Moore (discussed in the next chapter)—particularly his emphasis on the importance of building and maintaining strong relations with elected officials—gave Council leaders confidence in their new, more politically proactive approach. As a result, the Council moved from treating advocacy as a short-term crisis-response tactic to making an organizational commitment to long-term, strategic advocacy.

To emphasize that Council programs and activities support a wide spectrum of Montanans, Council leaders have encouraged individuals from outside the arts community to act as spokespersons for the agency. For example, the Council is working closely with the Montana Ambassadors, a volunteer organization that promotes Montana businesses, to spread the word about the many for-profit and nonprofit arts-related businesses that employ Montanans and provide them with products and services (Montana Arts Council, 2005).

A recurring theme in the Council's new approach to officials and the public has been the economic return to government investment in the arts. For example, the Council commissioned a statewide survey of arts nonprofit organizations in order to assess their impact on state tax revenues and employment (ArtsMarket, Inc., 2003). The study was distributed to officials within the Governor's Office and to state legislators, and the study results were widely reported by the media (Fitzgerald, 2003). Board members have also initiated opportunities to speak about the Council's work and to introduce local grantees and Council staff at service clubs and community events around the state.

Another feature of the Council's new approach is to expect more from grantees in making the case for public support of the arts to Montanans. Among other things, grantees are now required to (Montana Arts Council, 2002; RAND interviews)

---

[7] Montana's governor frequently solicits informal nominations for the Council's board from board members and the executive director.

- Maintain on their board of directors an active audience-development committee whose primary charge is to build participation with and for the organization;
- Designate a board member as responsible for identifying ways in which the grant has made a difference to the community and for helping the Council articulate the value of government support for the arts;
- Set up a meeting ("or have a coffee or a beer") with their legislators to discuss what the grant has meant to the community and to thank those legislators who support the Council;
- Assign responsibility for finding other ways to build relationships with legislators either to a newly established board committee or to the existing executive committee.

To some extent, these are not new expectations. Respondents reported that the Council has always asked grantees to emphasize audience development and to contribute to the Council's advocacy efforts. However, asking for specific commitments and making those commitments part of grantees' standard obligations are definite departures from past policy.

An additional component of the new approach to political leaders is the Listening Tour, a series of interviews designed to help the Council connect its programs and policies to the interests of those whose support is likely to be critical to the agency.[8] One or two interviewers, often including a board member, ask questions such as the following, none of which relates directly to the Council, its budget, or even the arts:

- What is the biggest concern you have for your town?
- How would you describe the types of people that drive your community?
- What convinces you that an activity or organization is worthy of state investment?

According to Council leaders, information gleaned from the Listening Tour will enable them to identify and point to Council programs and activities, and artists and arts organizations, that legislators and others will value and respect. One product that has already come out of the Tour is *Montana: The Land of Creativity* (Montana Arts Council, 2005), a publication that was distributed to every state legislator in 2005.[9] The publication highlights the Council's work in areas that legislators identified as important to them during interviews. For example, it highlights the state's need for creative thinkers and entrepreneurs and its need to create pride in Montana communities.

---

[8]   Appendix B provides more information on the Listening Tour, including the full list of questions.

[9]   The costs for this publication were jointly underwritten by The Wallace Foundation and a private nonprofit humanities group, the Montana Commission for the Humanities.

Respondents told us that in response to the governor's and legislators' strongly expressed interest in boosting Montana's economy, *Montana: The Land of Creativity* particularly emphasizes the economic return on public investment in Council programs.

It is still too early to tell whether these efforts will increase political support for the arts and the arts agency in the long term. Given the bruising and highly personal battle of 1997, the difficulties involved in achieving these outcomes should not be underestimated. But there is no question that the Council has won new friends in the legislature. In 2005, the Montana legislature restored $3.4 million to the Cultural Trust corpus, money that had been removed in 1997. And a March 2005 proposal to cut the Council's budget lost 82–18 in the Montana House of Representatives—the legislature instead reversed cuts that the governor had made (Fishbaugh, 2005a, 2005b). It seems clear that many more Montanans now view the Council's programs not as a drain on state resources, but as part of the solution to the state's economic and other problems.[10]

---

[10] See, for example, Harrington, 2004; Montana Arts Council, 2005.

CHAPTER FIVE

New Priorities for Public Arts Funding in Maine

The Maine Arts Commission was established in 1966 as an independent agency of state government, its mission to

> encourage and stimulate public interest and participation in the cultural heritage and cultural programs; expand the state's cultural resources; and encourage and assist freedom of artistic expression for the well being of the arts, to meet the needs and aspirations of persons in all parts of the state. (Maine Arts Commission, 2002d)

Like the Montana Arts Council, the Commission is a small SAA, with just nine full-time program staff. The executive director is hired by the board, which has up to 21 gubernatorial appointees. In FY 2004, the Commission's average legislative appropriation out of the state's general fund was approximately $878,000; per capita, Maine's legislative appropriation put the Commission at 29th of 50 SAAs.

Unlike the Montana Arts Council, however, the Commission's primary source of revenue is a legislative appropriation from Maine's general fund. Figure 5.1 shows the breakdown of the Commission's $1.6 million total revenue in FY 2004: the legislative appropriation accounted for 53 percent, money from private sources for 11 percent,[1] and grants from the NEA for 36 percent.[2]

Brief History of the Maine Arts Commission

The Commission was first established as the Maine State Commission on the Arts and Humanities, with $25,000 from the NEA and $10,000 from the state of Maine's general fund. By 1974, following tension between the humanities and arts programs, the

---

[1] Private funds were used mostly to support the Commission's Creative Economy initiative, discussed below.

[2] These are authors' calculations based on data provided by NASAA and the Maine Arts Commission. In Maine, funds for public art are not formally part of the Commission's budget and so are not included in revenue data. However, they are administered by the Commission and require some expenditure of Commission resources. In FY 2004, the budget for Maine's Percent for Art program came to roughly $300,000.

Figure 5.1
Revenue Sources for Maine Arts Commission, FY 2004

Total revenue: $1.6 million

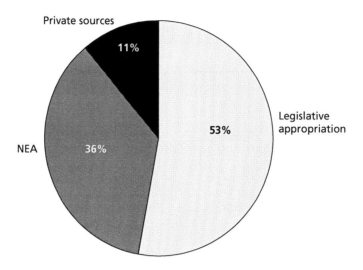

SOURCE: Authors' calculations based on data provided by NASAA
and the Maine Arts Commission.
RAND *MG359-5.1*

humanities program split off to become the independent nonprofit Maine Humanities
Council, leaving the Maine State Commission on the Arts and Humanities to focus
its efforts on arts programming (Wilson, 2004). At that time, the Commission joined
four other state cultural agencies under the umbrella of the Maine Department of
Educational and Cultural Services, which was commonly known as the Department
of Education. In 1986, the Commission's name was formally changed to the Maine
Arts Commission.

Like many SAAs, prior to the 1990s the Commission focused on competitive
grants to established arts institutions:

> Typical grants in the 1970s and 1980s included support for the exhibitions or per-
> formances of the Portland Symphony Orchestra, the Bangor Symphony Orchestra,
> the Portland Stage Company, the Portland Museum of Art, Bay Chamber Concerts
> in Rockport, Maine State Music Theater in Brunswick, and the Maine Maritime
> Museum in Bath. (Wilson, 2004, p. 242)

Some institutions received grants in excess of $20,000, a significant proportion of the
Commission's grantmaking budget. The majority of these institutions were in Portland,
Bangor, and various coastal cities and towns.

Respondents reported that in the 1960s and 1970s, positions on the Commission's 21-member board were predominantly ceremonial, and the governor appointed board members largely on the basis of their art-world credentials. The entire Commission—board members and staff—kept firmly out of the day-to-day political process. Commission leaders met with members of the state's legislative appropriations committee, for example, only when they were required to testify on behalf of their proposed budget, and they rarely met with legislators outside the budget cycle. There was no citizens' advocacy group for the arts, nor is there now.

In the 1980s, more politically oriented people were appointed to the board, and, as one respondent put it, "an activist became the chair." Encouraged by the new leadership, both staff and board members began seeking opportunities to raise their visibility with state legislators. For example, they initiated a program to showcase works by Maine artists in the state house rotunda—with conspicuous acknowledgment of the legislative districts in which each artist lived.[3] As a less formal approach, staff members were encouraged to walk through the state house during lunchtime, greeting legislators and telling them about Commission-sponsored activities in their districts.

By the end of the decade, the newly activist Commission had become frustrated with its position as part of the Department of Educational and Cultural Services because it felt its representation before the legislature was inadequate (Jorgensen, 2002). The other three state cultural agencies—the Maine State Library, the Maine Historic Preservation Commission, and the Maine State Museum—felt the same. In 1991, after an intensive information and advocacy campaign, the legislature separated the four from the Department of Educational and Cultural Services and formed a new umbrella organization, the Maine State Cultural Affairs Council (MCAC). Shortly thereafter, the Maine State Archives joined the new umbrella organization.[4] According to Jorgensen, MCAC's duties were "to coordinate budget requests, provide a forum for interagency planning and statewide cultural planning, and to be the formal liaison for interactions with other state agencies" (2002, p. 4).

Just a few years later, two events independently shook the Commission: a state fiscal crisis in which the governor targeted each of the state cultural agencies for cuts, and a severe NEA budget cut that resulted in the Commission losing most of its grant-

---

[3]   This Arts in the Capitol program has now expanded to include artwork displays in the Governor's Gallery (just outside the governor's office in the Maine Statehouse), Blaine House (the governor's official residence), the Legislative Gallery (by the main entrance to the building), and the Maine Arts Commission itself (Keyes, 2002).

[4]   The Maine State Archives remained under the Secretary of State's office but participated as an equal member in the policy decisions of MCAC (Jorgensen, 2002). Interestingly, two private nonprofit organizations, the Maine Humanities Council and the Maine Historical Society, became members of MCAC in 2001. In the case of the Humanities Council, it had come full circle, once again finding itself in partnership with the arts.

making funds.[5] During this tense period, Commission leaders realized they had to broaden and strengthen the agency's political support among elected officials and ordinary Mainers (RAND interviews). With their budget drastically reduced, they also had to rethink their entire portfolio of programs.

Maine's Strategy: Strengthening Communities, Strengthening Alliances

In the mid-1990s, Commission leaders held a series of carefully promoted public meetings around the state, a step that in itself represented a new direction for the Commission. Their goal was to find out what the Commission could do that would be of greatest value to Mainers given the drop in funds. After months of deliberation, they decided to all but abandon the role of grantmaker to large professional arts organizations.[6] Instead, they would focus their money and their efforts on "strengthening Maine communities through the arts and culture" (Maine Arts Commission, 1995). In practice, this meant the Commission would direct more resources, at least in relative terms, to individual artists, schools, and communities around the state. One staff member decided to leave the agency because of the change.

The reasons for the shift from professional arts organizations to artists and communities were described by our respondents as practical, philosophical, and political. For practical reasons, Commission leaders believed that small grants and technical assistance, which were all that they could now afford, would contribute more to the work of artists than to the work of large arts organizations. A philosophical reason for the shift was to achieve greater equity. Arts organizations in Maine tend to be clustered along the coast, whereas programs aimed at artists and communities are better able to reach the poorer, interior regions of the state.[7] Not coincidentally, it was also hoped that these new programs would raise the Commission's political visibility in areas of the state where the Commission had not been very active.

A key element in the Commission's new approach was to work more closely with its partners in MCAC. Commission leaders reported that one reason they chose to

---

[5] According to Commission managers, at this time the Commission was using mostly NEA money to fund its grant programs, and mostly state money to cover its administrative costs.

[6] Major organizations may still apply for a Governor's Award for Arts Accessibility, but this is a one-time grant that may be used only "for the purpose of hiring a professional consultant to complete an entire ADA [Americans with Disabilities Act] assessment of the physical facility and/or performance space(s)" (Maine Arts Commission, 2002a).

[7] For example, the Commission has had an Artists in the Schools program since 1969, but apparently there has never been enough money to satisfy demand. As described by our respondents, competition for grants under the old system was fierce, and winners tended to be coastal schools and artists. The Commission's new Partners in Arts and Learning program makes grants available by region on a three-year rotating basis, thereby ensuring that schools in the interior have access to arts education (Maine Arts Commission, 2002c).

begin by partnering with the other cultural agencies was simply that Maine's noncultural agencies at that time were not interested in what the Commission had to offer. In contrast, their MCAC partners saw artists as natural partners to libraries, historical museums, and heritage sites in community-building, and they all saw MCAC as the natural starting point for creating a politically effective constituency for the arts and culture. Meeting frequently to define common goals and priorities, the members of MCAC developed the concept for the New Century Community Program (NCCP), a program designed to

> strengthen local cultural resources including community arts activities, humanities programs and historic preservation activities; provide educational services beyond the reach of the standard K–12 educational system such as those offered through after school programs, cultural institutions, and non arts organizations; [and] preserve both the state's material culture and its built environment through grants for preservation and restoration. (Maine Arts Commission, 2002c)

MCAC then took the NCCP concept to the legislature in a joint budget request. The strategy worked: MCAC received a one-time appropriation of $3.2 million in the 1999 legislative session, $460,000 of which went to the Commission. In FY 2001, despite a serious state budget deficit, the program was reauthorized with an additional $1 million in funding (Maine Arts Commission, 2002b). Smaller amounts were authorized in 2002 and again in 2004, 2005, and 2006 (Maine Senate, Office of the President, 2005; RAND interviews). In addition, the legislature passed a capital construction bond issue of $1 million for arts and cultural facilities in July 2005.

A formal evaluation of the NCCP by Mt. Auburn Associates, Inc., in 2002 produced several important conclusions about what made it a political success for the agencies involved (Mt. Auburn Associates, 2002):

- The unified front presented by the coalition of cultural agencies made a strong, positive impact on legislators;
- The seven agencies were able to unite and mobilize their separate constituencies behind the NCCP;
- The proposal to distribute the funds widely across Maine garnered support in both rural and urban areas;
- The NCCP's initial status as a pilot program with one-time funding encouraged legislators to support it during its initial authorization and paved the way for the reauthorization;
- MCAC developed a coherent set of activities and outcomes that it highlighted during the authorizations process; and
- Requiring matching funds from other public and private sources was important in convincing legislators that the NCCP was an efficient use of state funds.

Interviews conducted for this report confirmed the evaluators' conclusions. Respondents stressed that a unified cultural front, combined constituencies, and geographic equity were all crucial to gaining Maine lawmakers' support for the NCCP. Several respondents also suggested that although funding for the NCCP per se has now diminished, statewide political support for the Commission is higher than it has ever been. They attribute this partly to the current governor, a former mayor of Bangor who believes the arts and culture have a big role to play in Maine's economic and community development. But they also believe it is the result of strategic groundwork carried out by the Commission and MCAC with the legislature and the public during the NCCP authorization and reauthorization campaigns.

In particular, respondents maintain that the NCCP has prepared the way for Maine's Creative Economy initiative, which has been spearheaded by the Commission. The governor launched the initiative with much fanfare in May 2004 and now has it as a cornerstone of his economic development strategy for the state (Maine Governor's Office, 2004). Items on the governor's policy agenda, which was formally introduced to the legislature in January 2005, include enhancement of arts education, strengthening of the state's universities and community-college system, financial support for an annual arts festival in Bangor, support for the NCCP, and financing for convention and cultural facilities (Maine Governor's Office, 2005). Under this governor and with this initiative, the Commission certainly seems to have secured a place at the table of state government.

CHAPTER SIX

Strategic Management of State Arts Agencies

The two SAAs examined in Chapters Four and Five, the Montana Arts Council and the Maine Arts Commission, show that it is possible for an arts agency to respond quickly and effectively to a major crisis. It is not immediately clear, however, to what extent the experiences—and strategies—of these two agencies apply to other SAAs. Both are small agencies in large but sparsely populated states that are, relative to many states, culturally homogeneous. And both Montana and Maine are "small government" states; that is, states in which public spending of all kinds is viewed with some suspicion. So are the experiences—and strategies—of these two SAAs relevant to SAAs located in heavily populated, highly diverse states that have a long tradition of public support for the arts?

We believe they are. Although the details vary, the Montana and Maine cases together illustrate some of the principles of strategic management identified in recent years in the literature on public administration. These principles, which emphasize the importance of strong agency leadership in achieving political support for an agency's mission, hold particular promise for government organizations that have operated at arm's length, such as SAAs.

Public-Value Framework

There has long been a debate in the field of public administration about the extent to which unelected government managers should be able to determine agency policies and decisions (Moore, 1995; Frederickson and Smith, 2003). One view is that such managers should restrict themselves to implementing the policies mandated by elected officials, who are in the best position to determine what is in the public interest (Wilson, 1887; Goodnow, 1900; Finer, 1936, 1941; Lowi, 1979). An opposing view is that as experts in their fields, these managers should use their judgment in deciding how their agencies can best serve the public (Friedrich, 1935, 1978 [1940]; Goodsell, 1983). In brief, the first group of scholars believes that the most important characteristic of a government manager is political responsiveness, and the second group emphasizes the benefits of managerial discretion.

In recent years, a new group of scholars has argued that the most successful government organizations are those whose leaders continuously seek a balance between political responsiveness and managerial discretion (Behn, 1991; Osborne and Gaebler, 1992; Barzelay, 1992). One member of this group, Mark H. Moore, is a professor at Harvard's Kennedy School of Government. In 2002, The Wallace Foundation asked him to introduce its START grantees to the strategic management concepts and tools he developed for other federal, state, and local government agencies. Presented as a series of workshops and telephone conferences, Moore's work was well received by the leaders of the 13 START SAAs—so much so, in fact, that it is now being introduced to other SAAs by NASAA and by regional arts service organizations such as Arts Midwest and WESTAF.

Moore's work has resonated with SAA leaders because, as discussed in previous chapters, SAAs have enjoyed considerable freedom to operate but little political visibility, and this situation has become a handicap. In the past, legislators established broad mandates for SAAs, gave them small budgets, and left them pretty much alone to pursue the public interest as they and the arts community saw fit. For the most part, neither legislators nor governors had much understanding of the public benefits of the arts and culture, but they did not need to as long as SAAs were heavily subsidized by federal grants.

But with states themselves now providing the bulk of SAA funding, this is no longer the case. In today's highly competitive state budget environment, SAA leaders not only must try to satisfy their arts community constituency, but also must convince elected officials that the arts can help them achieve their public policy priorities. Moore's work provides a language and a conceptual framework that help SAA leaders navigate this new world.

The Strategic Triangle

Figure 6.1 shows Moore's "strategic triangle," the image he uses to illustrate his concept (Moore and Moore, 2005). The triangle emphasizes three distinct issues he believes government managers must address if they are to create long-term value for the public and ensure their organization's survival: public value, legitimacy and support, and operational capacity.

Public value. To create the most value for residents, managers of government agencies need to identify a compelling mission and prioritize the goals they seek to achieve. The mission they choose must be consistent with the mandated purposes embodied in their agency's enabling legislation, but it need not be the same as the mission or missions they have pursued in the past. According to Moore and Moore (2005), "the material conditions and public aspirations of states change over time" (p. 25), so government managers should periodically reassess what would be most valuable for their agencies to do in light of those changes.

Figure 6.1
The Strategic Triangle

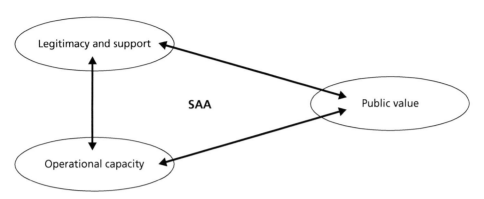

SOURCE: Used with permission of Moore and Moore, 2005.
RAND *MG359-6.1*

Legitimacy and support. Government managers also need to mobilize legitimacy and support from those who authorize the resources needed to carry out their agencies' work.[1] Moore argues that engaging with "political authorizers" (elected officials) is one of the primary responsibilities of all government managers. He stresses that managers should not focus their efforts solely on "known and trusted friends," but should reach out to their critics as well (Moore and Moore, 2005, p. 41). Additionally, he emphasizes that engagement involves listening as well as talking: Managers should not simply try to convince their authorizers that what they are doing is valuable; they should also attempt to find out what their authorizers believe would be valuable for them to do.[2]

Operational capacity. Finally, government managers must take stock of the assets and capacities at their disposal in order to identify missions and goals that are feasible and how to accomplish them most efficiently. Agency assets include the knowledge, skills, and connections of staff (and in the case of SAAs, board members), as well as relationships with external partners. For small agencies such as SAAs, Moore and Moore (2005) see partnerships as critical because "it is almost impossible [for small agencies] to achieve anything important entirely on [their] own" (p. 54).

In sum, Moore asserts that managers of the most successful government agencies are able to (1) make substantive judgments of what would be valuable and effective for their agency to do, (2) diagnose the political expectations of their agency, and (3) conduct hardheaded calculations of what is operationally feasible (Moore, 1995, p. 22). They do not take their agency's mission as given by the legislature, but neither do they

---

[1]   Included in this group of "authorizers" are people with influence over those who directly control resources; for example, politically powerful clients of the agency.

[2]   See, for example, Moore and Moore, 2005, p. 42.

define the agency's mission purely in terms of their own or their constituents' beliefs about what governmental priorities should be. Instead, they seek to create public value through an iterative process that takes into account the views of constituents—but also pays attention to the broader public and its elected representatives.

Through the Strategic Looking Glass: Montana and Maine

The strategic triangle provides a useful lens for examining our two case-study agencies. To overcome their immediate crises, agency leaders in Montana initially focused on mobilizing legitimacy and support from their political authorizers, whereas agency leaders in Maine sought to identify a compelling mission they could achieve with greatly reduced resources. We believe, however, that the most far-reaching effect of the crises in both agencies is likely to be a closer relationship with elected officials.

Public value. One of the most important steps that both the Montana Arts Council and the Maine Arts Commission took in response to their struggles during the 1990s was to systematically consider how their activities benefit all residents of their state and how best to communicate those benefits. Both agencies have reached out to the public and to legislators to discover what they most care about and have reexamined their programs in light of their findings.

This response is perhaps most clearly evident in the case of Maine, where, after the crisis, Commission board members initiated a series of statewide public meetings designed to reach out to residents not already benefiting from Commission programs. The meetings led to a new mission and new programs that distribute state arts money more equally around the state. Interestingly, Commission leaders believe that the new mission—to promote community development through the arts and culture—has moved the agency closer to its legislative mandate, which it had moved away from over the years. The new focus on communities has certainly pleased state legislators, who are strong proponents of geographic equity in arts funding (Mt. Auburn Associates, 2002).

In Montana, the Council's crisis experience did not result in explicit changes to its mission or programs, but it did prompt a new commitment to articulate the Council's value more effectively. As Council leaders point out, they have always distributed their grants fairly evenly around the state, and they believe a broad spectrum of Montana residents already view the agency's mission as important and worthwhile. They do not see a need to change their mission. Rather, they see their primary task as raising political leaders' awareness of the positive impact that the arts and, by extension, the agency have on Montanans.

Legitimacy and support. In fact, since the crisis, leaders of the Montana agency have been both systematic and strategic in garnering legitimacy and support for their agency. Building positive, personal relationships with state legislators is at the heart of their approach because, according to respondents, they were blindsided by legislators' indifference and even hostility to the agency during the 1997 crisis. In recognition of this, they are expanding their advocacy efforts beyond the circle of their friends by getting to know and be known by legislative leaders that have opposed the agency in the past. And because they believe a healthy economy is one of state government's highest priorities, their message to state legislators about Council programs consciously emphasizes the jobs and other economic benefits that the arts provide to the state.

The Maine agency's outreach to legislators has occurred mostly in the context of the NCCP and Creative Economy initiatives, both of which were introduced well after the budgetary crisis of the mid-1990s.[3] According to Jorgensen (2002), MCAC leaders (including leaders of the Commission) sought sponsorship for the initial NCCP legislation from a bipartisan, geographically diverse group of legislators. For reauthorization two years later, they had to educate a new set of legislators because Maine, like Montana, has term limits.[4] This process has continued, with recent efforts resulting in multiple legislative proposals to provide funding to the NCCP and Creative Economy, including a $25 million bond issue sponsored by the president of the Maine Senate and a $5 million bond issue sponsored by the governor (Maine Senate, Office of the President, 2005; RAND interviews).

Leaders at both the Montana and the Maine agency have also worked hard to strengthen relationships with their governors, which has not always been easy. Just as in other states, relations between the SAA and the governor tend to fluctuate with gubernatorial views about the importance of public arts funding. The governor of Maine throughout much of the 1990s, for example, did not see a strong role for the arts and culture in governmental planning for the future (RAND interviews). That is why MCAC decided to approach the legislature rather than the governor's office with its FY 1999 budget request for the NCCP (Jorgensen, 2002). It also contributed to MCAC's decision to host a candidates' forum on cultural affairs during the 2002 gubernatorial campaign.[5]

Montana's governors also have a mixed record on public support for the arts; but in 2002, Council leaders convinced the (now former) director of the Governor's Office of Economic Opportunity that arts-related businesses contribute substantively to the state's economy as well as to its quality of life (Harrington, 2004). As a result, under the previous governor, the "creative enterprise cluster" of for-profit and nonprofit cultural businesses featured prominently in Montana's economic development strategy (Montana Arts Council, 2005). A new governor was elected in 2004, however, and he has placed less emphasis on this strategy.

---

[3] This is not to say that legislators were kept in the dark about the changes at the Commission after its budget was cut. According to respondents, communications to legislators from community members enthusiastic about the changes far outnumbered communications from those who were upset.

[4] See Jorgensen, 2002, for a detailed and interesting account of how MCAC went about securing authorization for the NCCP in 1999 and reauthorization in 2001.

[5] The forum was attended by three of the four gubernatorial candidates (Maine Arts Commission, 2002d).

Finally, both agencies have crafted strategic alliances with other organizations in an effort to build political legitimacy and support.[6] In Montana, Council leaders decided that working with partners from outside the world of nonprofit arts and culture would help the agency—and the arts—shed an image of neediness. By joining forces with the Montana Economic Developers Association, the Montana State University Extension Service, and the Governor's Office of Economic Opportunity, they hope to dispel any lingering perceptions that nonprofit arts organizations are inherently different from other Montana businesses—or that artists are inherently different from other Montanans.[7] In Maine, the Commission's establishment of good working relations with other state cultural agencies, which began with the joint effort to break away from the Department of Education and create MCAC, was vital to the NCCP's success. The cultural coalition formed to make the case for the NCCP may be a model for other arts and culture advocacy efforts in the future.

Operational capacity. The Maine and Montana agencies also took stock of their operational capacities in the wake of their respective crises. In Montana, Council leaders cut the staff by 40 percent, eliminated the technical assistance and rural arts grant programs, and converted the annual "special project support" program for arts organizations to a biennial program that offers general operating support (RAND interviews). They did not, however, change their conception of the Council's major role (grantmaking) or its immediate clients (Montana nonprofit arts organizations) as a result of the crisis, believing they could carry out their mission even with reduced resources.

The Maine Arts Commission's crisis occurred in a less-hostile political environment than the Montana Arts Council's did, but the Commission's budgetary situation was actually worse in that the agency's capacity to carry out its existing mission was severely reduced. In recognition of this drastic reduction, the board members worked closely with the director to identify and adopt a new, operationally feasible mission for the Maine agency. As in Montana, the agency retained its primary role as grantmaker; but it did not retain its programs and activities, instead introducing new ones to fit its new mission.

Lessons from Montana and Maine

In sum, the SAAs in Montana and Maine in the mid-1990s found themselves in a crisis. In Montana, the agency was attacked by legislators and members of the public that were not only opposed to government support of the arts, but also highly critical

---

[6]   This is different from partnering with other agencies to provide services or administer programs. It involves jointly building a political constituency with another organization.

[7]   For example, the Council is working with the Montana Economic Developers Association to get community development professionals to incorporate the cultural sector (particularly nonprofit cultural organizations and artist-run businesses) into their plans for community development.

of artists and the arts community. In Maine, the rhetoric was less emotional but no less harmful to the agency. Legislators simply did not believe they should continue supporting the arts when the state budget was tight and residents were calling for smaller government.

In response to the crises, SAA leaders in Montana and Maine took a careful look at their agency's programs and activities to determine whether and, if so, how they

- Benefited state residents,
- Met the expectations of state elected officials, and
- Could be continued given the budgetary circumstances.

In Montana, SAA leaders decided that their agency's highest value lay in what it was already doing—helping arts organizations around the state to become more self-sufficient—and that it could and should keep on the same track. They therefore focused their efforts on connecting their work to the values and priorities of state legislators. In Maine, SAA leaders concluded that many state residents were not benefiting from their agency's activities, and that even fewer would benefit after the budget cuts. They thus chose to eliminate their organizational support program in order to focus their resources on artists and communities around the state, a decision that offended some arts organizations but gained the support of legislators from rural districts.

An important lesson from the Montana and Maine experiences is that there is no one-size-fits-all approach to serving the residents of different states through the arts. Each agency must decide for itself whether it has identified a compelling mission and whether it can carry that mission out. But it is also important to note that although the substance of the two agencies' responses to a crisis differed, the strategies employed were alike in that they resonated with the political leaders and publics of each state.

Further, even though the Montana agency has focused on developing personal relationships with legislators and the Maine agency has focused on creating a broad-based cultural coalition, the advocacy strategies of the two agencies have four important elements in common:

- Making good use of the knowledge, skills, and connections of directors and board members to raise the agency's visibility with elected officials and the public;
- Identifying ways in which their programs and activities benefit residents who are not regular participants in the arts;
- Ensuring a degree of geographic equity in agency programs and activities; and
- Convincing state government leaders that their programs and activities align with state government priorities.

Relevance of Lessons to Other States

For both the Montana and the Maine SAA, this new, arm-in-arm approach to political leaders grew out of an immediate crisis. However, because the current political and budgetary trends (see Chapter Three) are affecting all SAAs to differing degrees, SAA leaders in many states are seeking to mobilize legitimacy and support for their agencies.

A number of SAAs have recognized that disengaged or politically isolated boards are a liability in the current arts funding environment. They are therefore clarifying what it is they want from their board members, asking them to assume more leadership with respect to policymaking and advocacy. The Massachusetts Cultural Council, for example, informs all new board members of their ultimate responsibility for defining and articulating the agency's mission. In Arizona, new board members are asked to sign a statement promising to "interpret the organization's work and values to the community" and "further the Commission's goals by speaking with elected officials, and participating in advocacy opportunities."[8] And eight SAAs have formally adopted the ideas of John Carver, an expert in the area of board-based governance whose works offer, for example, ideas on how to help boards focus on policy issues, refrain from micro-management, and rigorously evaluate the goals and accomplishments of their organizations (Carver, 1990; and Carver and Carver, 2004).[9]

Some SAAs have also sharpened their focus on how to better serve the residents of their states. As in Maine, several SAAs are reaching out to new constituents through expanded strategic planning efforts.[10] For example, the South Carolina Arts Commission's 2001 Canvas of the People forums entailed "a telephone survey of 800 South Carolinians eighteen and older to establish a snapshot of arts awareness and involvement among the state's general population" (South Carolina Arts Commission, 2001, p. 4), followed by a series of public forums to supplement the survey information. In Ohio, the State of the Arts Report survey effort was intended to ensure that the arts agency's "guidelines and policies [are] formed from a realistic depiction of the arts and culture in Ohio, rather than on assumptions about the makeup of Ohio's arts community" (Ohio Arts Council, 2001, p. 5).

Almost 30 SAAs have responded to legislators' concerns about geographic equity by providing block grants to local or regional arts agencies or country governments for

---

[8]   Quoted from unpublished materials sent to the authors from the Massachusetts Cultural Council and the Arizona Commission on the Arts, April 2005.

[9]   The eight states are Colorado, Hawaii, Kansas, Kentucky, Mississippi, New York, Tennessee, and Vermont (2000–2001 NASAA Profile Survey; April 2005 review of SAA Websites).

[10]   According to several respondents, SAA strategic planning processes in the past were often "insider" efforts, involving individuals who were quite close to the agency.

regranting.[11] Of these, 13 use a population-based formula for allocating their decentralization program funds.[12] Several SAAs try to ensure that grants are widely distributed by establishing programs that specifically target underserved constituents or areas.[13] Still others, as in Maine, have made the equitable geographic distribution of grants a review criterion for certain programs.

Finally, as in both Montana and Maine, several SAAs are now seeking to align their missions and goals with the policy agendas of state elected leaders. The North Carolina Arts Council, for example, recently reexamined its mission statement and goals in light of the statements and goals of other state government organizations, most notably the governor's office. The agency's leaders wished to see which public values other agencies identified as most important. As a result of their review, they chose a new mission statement ("to make North Carolina a better state through the arts") and decided that the primary goal of their work would be to promote vibrant communities, creative and productive citizens, and the state's cultural vitality (North Carolina Arts Council, 2005).

Arm in Arm with State Government Leaders?

In responding to the new political and economic environment, most SAA leaders have not chosen to substantively change their missions. Instead, they have sought to mobilize political legitimacy and support for their agencies by casting existing programs and activities in a new light. Although they point to the benefits their activities bring to a wide spectrum of state residents, they are not taking funding from existing constituents in order to broaden the spectrum or magnify the benefits.

One explanation for why SAAs are not choosing to change their missions may be that the easiest course when faced with vocal and insistent grantees and supporters is simply to maintain the status quo. For some SAAs, this explanation is probably correct, although it is not likely to remain the easiest course for long. For other SAAs, it

---

[11] This is the authors' calculation based on available information (NASAA, 1992a; 2000–2001 NASAA Profile Survey; September 2005 review of SAA Websites). In Massachusetts, Minnesota, New York, and North Carolina, decentralization programs were legislatively mandated in the 1970s; the Texas state legislature mandated a decentralization program for its SAA in 1992.

[12] The 13 SAAs that use population-based formulas to allocate funds to regranting agencies are Georgia, Illinois, Indiana, Louisiana, Maryland, Massachusetts, Michigan, Minnesota, New York, North Carolina, Pennsylvania, Tennessee, and Texas (NASAA, 1992a; NASAA, 1995; September 2005 review of SAA Websites).

[13] For example, the Ohio Arts Council and West Virginia Commission on the Arts' joint Ohio River Border Initiative makes funds available for "artists, arts groups and community arts programs in all Ohio and West Virginia counties that touch the Ohio River" (Ohio Arts Council, n.d.).

may be that they have examined their activities and, like Montana's agency, have concluded that better communication is all they need to gain the support of state political leaders.

Some SAA leaders, however, are still thinking deeply about what a more compelling mission for their agencies might look like.[14] One question they must address is the extent to which they should actually allow their programs to be shaped by the interests and concerns of state officials, as opposed to the interests and concerns of the arts community or even the general public. Are the rewards associated with bringing the arts and political worlds closer together worth the risks? Once again, the Montana and Maine experiences offer some insights.

---

[14] See, for example, the discussions in Radich, 2003.

CHAPTER SEVEN

At Arm's Length . . . But Dancing

Our research suggests that Moore's strategic triangle—specifically, the idea of mobilizing political legitimacy and support—has resonated strongly with SAA leaders. SAAs across the country have identified ways in which their programs and activities benefit residents in their states. They have also adopted more-proactive approaches to advocacy. In Montana and Maine, the SAAs' realistic analyses of and creative responses to their political and budgetary environments have put the two agencies on a firmer political footing after near-elimination in the 1990s.

Risks of Arm-in-Arm Approaches

But the experiences of the Montana Arts Council and the Maine Arts Commission also point to some risks that may be associated with lowering the barriers between art and politics. One such risk is that closer relations with elected officials will make SAAs dependent on political friendships. Some of our respondents claim, for example, that the success of Maine's Creative Economy initiative has depended heavily on close friendships between individual board members and the governor. Some also suggest that the Commission is now too closely associated with a particular political party. According to these respondents, the next governor may choose to ignore the arts in an effort to distance his or her policies from those of the current administration.

A related concern is that SAAs may become too cozy with their political authorizers. For example, a few of our Montana respondents feel that the Montana Arts Council has compromised its artistic focus in trying to please elected officials. These critics point to changes in the composition of the board, arguing that without representation from artists or arts organizations, the Council lacks perspective on the arts. Some also express concern over a trend toward supporting the more commercial "Western heritage" art over classical or contemporary art. Others cite the discontinuation of the Artists Fellowships program as an indication of the Council's more conservative bent and reluctance to support challenging art.[1]

A broader concern is that agency leaders will justify public support of the arts entirely in terms of instrumental benefits, such as economic development and improved education. They will then lose sight of what makes the arts uniquely rewarding.[2] Consider the case of Montana, where the Council leaders' case for public support in the troubled state economy rests primarily on the impact of the arts on economic development, tourism, and jobs.[3] Some interview respondents think that characterizing the arts as a conduit for economic development may eventually become a liability for the Council. If art is oversold as an economic panacea, they argue, artists and arts groups may lose out to other, non-arts groups that can point to even larger economic returns on state government investment. In the process, the Council will have compromised the arts community's core value to the people of Montana—the value of its art as art. In the view of these respondents, the Council's business-oriented approach has another drawback in that it risks alienating those members of the arts community whose support is vital to achieving its mission.

Too much focus on the instrumental benefits of the arts is also a concern in Maine. Some respondents argue that the Creative Economy initiative has received a large amount of attention only because of that state's severe economic difficulties. With the eventual election of a new governor and an improvement in the economy, they believe, state government officials will once again focus on their traditional areas of interest, which do not include the arts. When this happens, they fear, the Commission, and the arts, will once again be relegated to the margins of state government.

Finally, several respondents also raise a question familiar to the arts, that of excellence versus access. Some argue, for example, that the Maine Arts Commission's new mission has led it to sprinkle public money on mediocre artists and artworks throughout the state. A related criticism is that the Commission has abandoned the leading

---

[1]   In response to the criticism, Montana agency leaders point out that there *are* artists on the Council's board, as well as board members who represent arts organizations. They suggest that perhaps these artists and arts organizations are simply not the ones their critics would have chosen. The Council did discontinue its Artists Fellowships program when it instituted its new approach to authorizers. However, according to Council leaders, the program was discontinued not to please or placate elected officials, but because, at roughly five fellowships per year, it was simply not serving enough people.

[2]   McCarthy et al., 2005, summarizes current theories about the instrumental and the intrinsic benefits of the arts and discusses shortcomings associated with economic and other instrumental rationales for public arts support.

[3]   See, for example, Montana Arts Council, 2005. Council leaders reply that Council programs and activities offer a host of benefits to Montana residents, and that they are happy to point to all of them. They have found it constructive, however, to emphasize certain benefits to certain audiences, and public officials in Montana seem to care most about the economic benefits of the arts.

segment of the Maine arts community, the major arts organizations.[4] Some respondents believe the Commission's lack of support for the major arts organizations will come back to haunt it politically in the future.

On the question of excellence, or quality, leaders from both agencies are adamant that they have made no sacrifices. They believe that extremely good artists can be found throughout their states, even in the remoter rural areas. The real challenge is choosing among them. In Maine, SAA leaders further argue that participation in the arts at the community level helps build audiences for the state's major arts organizations. Our interviews suggest that most of the major arts organizations do not agree with this argument. However, one director of a major institution did express support for programs such as the NCCP. He believes that in the long run, the Commission's focus on schools and communities will create more demand for the artistic products of major institutions such as his.

Rewards of Arm-in-Arm Approaches

The issues that arise with arm-in-arm approaches are important and should be debated within SAAs and by all those who believe in public support for the arts. They show that managing an SAA, just like managing any government organization, is a complex responsibility. SAA leaders must be responsive to multiple needs and interests, including those of the arts community, the general public, and elected political leaders.

Given the prevailing economic and political trends described in Chapter Three, however, SAA leaders have little choice but to work more closely with state political leaders. As we have seen, state appropriations have assumed an increasing proportion of SAA budgets but their future growth is by no means assured. If SAAs do not raise their visibility with those who authorize their resources, they risk further marginalizing their agencies within their states. Recent developments in Europe illustrate what can happen to arm's-length arts agencies: In Wales and Scotland, political leaders are threatening to take over much of the arts agencies' decisionmaking authority.[5] SAA

---

[4]   The Commission offers technical assistance to arts organizations in such areas as strategic planning, evaluation, and capital campaigns. But this type of assistance may not be useful to major institutions, which are typically already quite sophisticated in these areas. According to respondents, what the majors want is general operating support, a type of program the Commission is unlikely to reinstitute in the foreseeable future.

[5]   For example, the Welsh Assembly very narrowly rejected a plan to fund the six largest performing arts organizations in Wales directly, rather than through the Arts Council of Wales. The Scottish Executive also intends to take on direct funding of the arts, and is reportedly considering a statutory duty on local authorities in order to ensure the equitable distribution of public arts funding ("Arts Row Rings English Alarm Bells," 2006; MacDonnell, 2006).

leaders must therefore find ways to justify their agencies' programs, and they (as well as others who believe in public support for the arts) must recognize that instrumental arguments appear to be most able to persuade state political leaders.

Our case studies, which we offer as illustrations of a strategic approach to public management, suggest that the rewards of arm-in-arm approaches outweigh the risks. By opening a conversation with state political leaders, SAA leaders can learn about their priorities and at the same time help them understand how the arts can contribute to achieving their priorities.

But it is important to emphasize that SAA leaders are not passive participants in this conversation. While paying close attention to the priorities of state residents and political leaders, they also have the opportunity to influence those priorities. So far, it is SAA leaders, not politicians, who are responsible for their agencies' policies and programs. If they can work with state government leaders without being dominated by them, all state residents will benefit from more stable public funding of the arts and a greater integration of the arts and culture into governmental planning for the future.

Some Facts About State Arts Agencies

Agency	Date Founded	2005 Legislative Appropriation (net line items) ($)	2005 Total Revenue (including line items) ($)	2005 Total Revenue Per Capita ($)	Type of Board / Requirement for Legislators to Serve on Council or Panels
Alabama Arts Council	1966	3,169,195	3,835,995	0.85	Governing / No
Alaska State Council on the Arts	1966	461,300	1,061,400	1.64	Governing / No
Arizona Commission on the Arts	1966	3,522,727	4,372,327	0.78	Governing / No
Arkansas Arts Council	1971	1,460,643	2,064,743	0.76	Governing / No
California Arts Council	1963	1,968,000	3,145,100	0.09	Governing / No
Colorado Council on the Arts	1967	500,000	1,139,000	0.25	Governing / No
Connecticut Commission on Culture and Tourism	1965	3,779,939	15,917,328	4.57	Governing / No
Delaware Division of the Arts	1969	1,708,900	2,377,620	2.91	Advisory / No
Florida Division of Cultural Affairs	1966	15,809,390	16,491,790	0.97	Advisory / No
Georgia Council for the Arts	1964	3,799,735	4,421,846	0.51	Governing / No
Hawaii State Foundation on Culture and the Arts	1965	5,416,236	6,646,336	5.28	Governing / No
Idaho Commission on the Arts	1966	822,800	1,488,450	1.09	Governing / No
Illinois Arts Council	1963	12,579,000	19,544,100	1.54	Governing / No
Indiana Arts Council	1965	3,617,337	4,221,937	0.68	Governing / No
Iowa Arts Council	1967	1,349,586	1,909,786	0.65	Advisory/No
Kansas Arts Commission	1966	1,516,857	2,223,323	0.82	Governing / No
Kentucky Arts Council	1966	3,593,700	4,253,600	1.03	Governing / No
Louisiana Division of the Arts	1965	5,066,961	5,898,461	1.31	Advisory / No

Agency	Date Founded	2005 Legislative Appropriation (net line items) ($)	2005 Total Revenue (including line items) ($)	2005 Total Revenue Per Capita ($)	Type of Board / Requirement for Legislators to Serve on Council or Panels
Maine Arts Commission	1966	814,737	1,424,937	1.09	Governing / No
Maryland State Arts Council	1966	11,001,522	11,854,122	2.15	Governing / Yes
Massachusetts Cultural Council	1966	8,346,874	9,588,964	1.49	Governing / No
Michigan Council for Arts and Cultural Affairs	1966	11,774,100	12,450,650	1.24	Governing / No
Minnesota State Arts Board	1961	8,593,000	9,970,800	1.97	Governing / No
Mississippi Arts Commission	1968	1,661,551	5,426,004	1.88	Governing / No
Missouri Arts Council	1962	500,000	4,125,116	0.72	Governing / No
Montana Arts Council	1967	292,465	1,639,324	1.79	Governing / No
Nebraska Arts Council	1965	1,035,834	2,355,197	1.35	Governing / No
Nevada Arts Council	1967	1,475,576	2,403,393	1.07	Governing / No
New Hampshire State Council on the Arts	1965	691,465	1,382,865	1.07	Advisory / No
New Jersey State Council on the Arts	1966	23,180,000	29,961,719	3.47	Governing / Yes
New Mexico Arts	1965	1,358,000	2,076,100	1.11	Advisory / No
New York State Council on the Arts	1960	42,321,000	45,242,800	2.36	Governing / No
North Carolina Arts Council	1964	5,311,036	6,887,772	0.82	Advisory / No
North Dakota Council on the Arts	1967	502,202	1,090,102	1.72	Governing / No
Ohio Arts Council	1965	11,375,734	12,444,300	1.09	Governing / Yes
Oklahoma Arts Council	1965	3,878,871	4,664,056	1.33	Governing / No
Oregon Arts Commission	1967	584,337	1,475,602	0.41	Governing / No
Pennsylvania Council on the Arts	1966	14,500,000	15,289,700	1.24	Governing / Yes
Rhode Island State Council on the Arts	1967	1,441,641	3,317,064	3.08	Governing / No
South Carolina Arts Commission	1967	2,833,265	4,077,221	0.98	Governing / No
South Dakota Arts Council	1967	588,481	1,218,181	1.59	Governing / No
Tennessee Arts Commission	1965	1,789,900	6,513,400	1.11	Governing / No
Texas Commission on the Arts	1965	4,510,252	5,745,866	0.26	Governing / No
Utah Arts Council	1899	2,499,700	3,310,700	1.41	Governing / No

Agency	Date Founded	2005 Legislative Appropriation (net line items) ($)	2005 Total Revenue (including line items) ($)	2005 Total Revenue Per Capita ($)	Type of Board / Requirement for Legislators to Serve on Council or Panels
Vermont Arts Council	1965	494,618	1,523,000	2.46	Governing / No
Virginia Commission for the Arts	1968	3,001,535	3,647,435	0.49	Governing / No
Washington State Arts Council	1965	2,274,200	5,267,149	0.86	Governing / Yes
West Virginia Division of Culture and History	1967	1,127,718	6,015,044	3.32	Advisory / No
Wisconsin Arts Board	1973	2,159,800	2,811,200	0.51	Governing / No
Wyoming Arts Council	1967	547,494	1,107,994	2.21	Advisory / No
TOTAL		242,609,214	327,320,919	1.10	

SOURCES: NASAA, 2005; NASAA Profile Survey 2000–2001; NEA 1978; SAA Websites.

Montana Arts Council's Listening Tour

The first step of the Montana Arts Council's Listening Tour interview process, begun in 2003, was to identify and prioritize individuals to be interviewed. Five categories of authorizers (that is, the people who authorize the resources needed to carry out the agency's work and those with influence over those resources) were identified: (1) leaders within the state legislature and candidates for the leadership; (2) the governor, candidates for governor, and members of the governor's staff; (3) economic development leaders (for example, presidents of local chambers of commerce); (4) officials from the Montana Department of Commerce and Travel Montana; (5) U.S. Congressional representatives and their staffs.

Interviews with Montana political leaders were structured around five themes, for a total of 16 questions:

Elected official as a citizen
1. What do you value most about living in Montana?
2. How would you describe the character of your community?
3. Is there a part of your community fabric that has you really engaged in terms of giving your time or donating materials or money?
4. Why did that engagement begin?
5. What is the biggest threat to or biggest concern you have for your town?

What is good citizenship?
6. Do you have an example of a successful "citizen" of your town?
7. What makes that person a successful citizen of your community?
8. How would you describe the types of people that drive your community?

What is public service?
9. What brought you to public service?
10. What led you to choose your political party?
11. What do you believe is your chief responsibility as a public official?

What is public value?
12. How would you define public value?
13. What role does public value play in how you make your decisions as a public official?

14. Has your definition of public value changed since you first took office/began running your campaign?

Connecting public value to creative enterprise (the arts)

15. How much value to the state's future do you place on creativity?

16. Do you recall having a creative or an arts experience that made a significant impression on you?

Bibliography

Adams, Don, and Arlene Goldbard, *Cultural Policy in U.S. History*, essay adapted from unpublished 1986 manuscript, 1995. Available at http://www.wwcd.org/policy/US/UShistory.html (as of April 14, 2006).

Adams, William Howard, *The Politics of Arts: Forming a State Arts Council*, New York: Arts Councils of America, 1966.

Americans for the Arts, *Local Arts Agency Facts 2000*, Washington, D.C.: Americans for the Arts, 2001.

Arey, June Batten, *State Arts Agencies in Transition: Purpose, Program, and Personnel*, Wayzata, MN: Spring Hill Conference Center, 1975.

Arian, Edward, *The Unfulfilled Promise: Public Subsidy of the Arts in America*, Philadelphia, PA: Temple University Press, 1989.

Armbrust, Roger, "Congress Ekes Out NEA Raise," *Backstage.com News East*, 9 December 2004. Available at http://www.backstage.com.

"Arts Row Rings English Alarm Bells," *Western Mail*, 7 January 2006. Available at http://icwales.icnetwork.co.uk/0900entertainment/0050artsnews/tm_objectid=16557056%26method=full%26siteid=50082-name_page.html (as of April 14, 2006).

ArtsMarket, Inc., "The Role of Non-Profit Arts Organizations in Montana's Economy," Bozeman, MT: ArtsMarket, Inc., 2003.

Avner, Marcia, *The Lobbying and Advocacy Handbook for Nonprofit Organizations: Shaping Public Policy at the State and Local Level*, St. Paul, MN: Minnesota Council of Nonprofits, 2002.

Backas, James, "The State Arts Council Movement," unpublished background paper prepared for the National Partnership Meeting, The George Washington University, Washington, D.C., 23–25 June 1980.

Barsdate, Kelly, "The State Arts Agency Policy Environment," working paper, University of Chicago Cultural Policy Center, April 2001.

Barsdate, Kelly, "Public Funding for the Arts," presentation prepared for the Foundation Center's Funding for Arts Month, June 2003.

Barzelay, Michael, *Breaking Through Bureaucracy: A New Vision for Managing in Government*, Berkeley, CA: University of California Press, 1992.

Behn, Robert D., *Leadership Counts: Lessons for Public Managers from the Massachusetts Welfare, Training, and Employment Program*, Cambridge, MA: Harvard University Press, 1991.

Betty, Sam, "Trust Issues in the Relationship Between State Arts Agencies and Arts-Advocacy Groups: A Preliminary Report," unpublished paper prepared for the Western States Arts Federation, December 2002.

"Block Attack on Arts," editorial, *Great Falls Tribune*, 31 January 1999, p. 6A.

California Arts Council (CAC), *2001 Public Opinion Survey*, Sacramento, CA: CAC, 2001.

California Governor's Office, *A Government for the People for a Change: Governor's Reorganization Plan 1: Reforming California's Boards and Commissions*, Sacramento, CA: Governor's Office, 2005.

Carver, John, *Boards That Make a Difference: A New Design for Leadership in Nonprofit and Public Organizations*, San Francisco, CA: Jossey-Bass Publishers, 1990.

Carver, John, and Miriam Carver, "The Policy Governance Model," 2004. Available at http://www.carvergovernance.com/model.htm (as of April 14, 2006).

Center for Nonprofit Management, "Frequently Asked Questions About Lobbying and Advocacy by Nonprofits," 2004. Available at http://www.cnmsocal.org/ForNonprofits/FAQLobbying.html (as of April 14, 2006).

Chartrand, Harry H., and Claire McCaughey, "The Arm's Length Principle and the Arts: An International Perspective—Past, Present and Future," in Milton C. Cummings and J. Mark Schuster, eds., *Who's to Pay for the Arts? The International Search for Models of Support*, New York: ACA Books, 1989, pp. 43–80.

Cummings, Milton C., Jr., "Government and the Arts: An Overview," in Stephen Benedict, ed., *Public Money and the Muse*, New York: W.W. Norton, 1991, pp. 31–79.

Cwi, David, "Arts Councils as Public Agencies: The Policy Impact of Mission, Role and Operations," in William S. Hendon and James L. Shanahan, eds., *Economics of Cultural Decision*, Cambridge, MA: Abt Books, 1983, pp. 38–46.

Devlin, Graham, and Sue Hoyle, *Committing to Culture: Arts Funding in France and Britain*, London: Franco-British Council British Section, 2000.

DiMaggio, Paul J., and Toquir Mukhtar, "Arts Participation as Cultural Capital in the United States, 1982–2002: Signs of Decline?" *Poetics*, Vol. 32, No. 2, April 2004, pp. 169–194.

DiMaggio, Paul J., and Becky Pettit, "Public Opinion and Political Vulnerability: Why Has the National Endowment for the Arts Been Such an Attractive Target?" Working Paper No. 7, Center for Arts and Cultural Policy Studies, Princeton, NJ: Princeton University, January 1999.

Dworkin, Dennis, "State Advocacy and the Arts: A Historical Overview," *Journal of Arts Management and Law*, Vol. 21, No. 3, Fall 1991, pp. 199–214.

Finer, Herman, "Better Government Personnel," *Political Science Quarterly*, Vol. 51, 1936, pp. 569–599.

Finer, Herman, "Administrative Responsibility in Democratic Government," 1941. Reprinted in F.E. Rourke, ed., *Bureaucratic Power in National Politics*, 3rd edition, Boston, MA: Little, Brown, 1978, pp. 176–187.

Fishbaugh, Arlynn, "Senate Restores Arts Council Budget; Legislature Restores Cultural Trust Corpus," *State of the Arts Newspaper*, Montana Arts Council, May/June 2005a.

Fishbaugh, Arlynn, Montana Arts Council, "Legislature Restores Rest of MAC Budget," *State of the Arts Newspaper*, Montana Arts Council, July/August 2005b.

Fitzgerald, John, "Economic Effect of Arts Detailed," *The Billings Gazette*, 28 May 2003.

Frederickson, H. George, and Kevin B. Smith, *The Public Administration Theory Primer*, Boulder, CO: Westview Press, 2003.

Free Expression Policy Project, New York University School of Law, *Free Expression in Arts Funding: A Public Policy Report*, 2003. Available at http://www.fepproject.org/policyreports/artsfunding.pdf (as of April 14, 2006).

Freeman, Robert, "Why Do We Make Music and Art?" moderator's essay for the television series *Closer to Truth*, Show 206, broadcast October 2000.

Friedrich, Carl J., "Responsible Government Service Under the American Constitution," in C.J. Friedrich, W.C. Beyer, S.D. Sporo, J.F. Miller, and G.A. Graham, eds., *Problems of the American Public Service*, 1935.

Friedrich, Carl J., "Public Policy and the Nature of Administrative Responsibility," 1940. Reprinted in F.E. Rourke, ed., *Bureaucratic Power in National Politics*, 3rd edition, Boston, MA: Little, Brown, 1978, pp. 165–175.

Galligan, Ann M., "The Politicization of Peer-Review Panels at the NEA," in J. H. Balfe, ed., *Paying the Piper: Causes and Consequences of Arts Patronage*, Urbana and Chicago, IL: University of Illinois Press, 1993.

Garrett, Thomas A., and Gary A. Wagner, "State Government Finances: World War II to the Present," *Federal Reserve Bank of St. Louis Review*, Vol. 86, No. 2, March/April 2004, pp. 9–25.

General Accounting Office, *Unfunded Mandates: Analysis of Reform Act Coverage*, GAO-04-637, May 2004.

Goodnow, Frank, *Politics and Administration: A Study in Government*, New York: Russell and Russell, 1900.

Goodsell, Charles, *The Case for Bureaucracy: A Public Administration Polemic*, Chatham, NJ: Chatham House, 1983.

Guinane, Pat, "Culture Cash," *Illinois Issues*, December 2005.

Harrington, John, "Spurring a Western Economy: State Explores the Economics of Art," *Helena Independent Record*, November–December 2004.

Harris, John S., "Arts Councils: A Survey and Analysis," *Public Administration Review*, July/August 1970, pp. 387–399.

Hedge, David M., *Governance and the Changing American States*, Boulder, CO: Westview Press, 1998.

Hernandez, Rick, "Future Scenarios for State Arts Agencies: The Texas Perspective," in A. Radich et al., eds., *Re-envisioning State Arts Agencies*, proceedings of a symposium held by the Western States Arts Federation, Denver, CO, 17–19 October 2003, pp. 43–47.

Hessenius, Barry, "California: What Might Be Next?" in A. Radich et al., eds., *Re-envisioning State Arts Agencies*, proceedings of a symposium held by the Western States Arts Federation, Denver, CO, 17–19 October 2003, pp. 53–55.

Hoekstra, Pete, *A Creative and Generous America: The Healthy State of the Arts in America and the Continued Failure of the National Endowment of the Arts*, Chairman's Report, U.S. House Committee on Education and the Workforce, Subcommittee on Oversight and Investigations, 23 September 1997.

Hogwood, Brian W., "The 'Growth' of Quangos: Evidence and Explanations," *Parliamentary Affairs*, Vol. 48, 1995, pp. 207–225.

Holman, Rhonda, "Art for Our Sake: Candidates Support for NEA Has Been Weak at Best," *St. Paul Pioneer Press*, 10 October 2000.

Hurdle, Joan, "The 1999 Legislature and the Arts," Representative, Montana Legislature, House District 13, 24 July 2000.

Indiana Arts Commission, *Policy Manual for the Indiana Arts Commission*, Indianapolis, IN: Indiana Arts Commission, 2004a.

Indiana Arts Commission, *Two-Year Grant Program for Multi-Regional Major Arts Institutions: Sample Guidelines*, Indianapolis, IN: Indiana Arts Commission, 2004b.

Institute of Governmental Studies Library, University of California, Berkeley, "Boards and Commissions in California State Government," February 2005. Available at http://www.igs.berkeley.edu/library/htCABoardsCommissions.html (as of April 14, 2006).

Jorgensen, Erik, "From Concept to Authorization: A History of the Maine New Century Community Program," in Mt. Auburn Associates, Inc., *The New Century Community Program: An Evaluation and Case Study of State Arts and Cultural Policy*, final report, Cambridge, MA: Mt. Auburn Associates, August 2002.

Kettl, Donald F., *Reinventing Government: A Fifth-Year Report Card*, Center for Public Management Report CPM 98-1, Washington, D.C.: Brookings Institution, September 1998.

Keyes, Bob, "Maine Art . . . With a Capitol Audience," *Portland Press Herald*, 22 December 2002.

Kreidler, John, "Leverage Lost: The Non-Profit Arts in the Post-Ford Era," *Journal of Arts Management, Law, and Society*, Vol. 36, No. 2, 1996.

Larmer, Paul, Kathie Durbin, Todd Wilkinson, Tony Davis, Steve Stuebner, and Jon Christensen, "Goodbye, New West; Hello Lords of Yesterday: Dispatches from the Field," *High Country News: Western Roundup*, Vol. 26, No. 22, 28 November 1994.

Larson, Gary O., *The Reluctant Patron: The United States Government and the Arts, 1943–65*, Philadelphia, PA: University of Pennsylvania Press, 1983.

Larson, Gary O., *American Canvas*, Washington, D.C.: NEA, 1997.

Little Hoover Commission, "Boards and Commissions: California's Hidden Government," Report presented to the Governor and Members of the Legislature by the Commission on California State Government Organization and Economy, 18 July 1989.

Lowell, Julia F., *State Arts Agencies 1965–2003: Whose Interests to Serve?* MG-121-WF, Santa Monica, CA: RAND Corporation, 2004.

Lowi, Theodore, *The End of Liberalism*, New York: W.W. Norton, 1979.

MacDonnell, Hamish, "Executive to Be Cultural Caretaker as It Takes on Arts Funding," *The Scotsman*, 16 January 2006.

Maine Arts Commission, "Five Year Strategic Plan 1996–2001," Augusta, ME: Maine Arts Commission, 1995.

Maine Arts Commission, "Governor's Award for Arts Accessibility," 2002a. Available at http://www.mainearts.com/organizations/Accessibility/index.shtml (as of April 14, 2006).

Maine Arts Commission, "Partners in Arts and Learning," 2002b. Available at http://mainearts.maine.gov/organizations/education/pal.shtml (as of April 14, 2006).

Maine Arts Commission, "New Century Community Program," 2002c. Available at http://www.mainearts.com/organizations/newcentury/index.shtml (as of April 14, 2006).

Maine Arts Commission, "The Art of Politics: What Does Maine's Next Governor Say in Support of the Arts & Culture?" *MaineArts Mag*, Fall 2002d.

Maine Governor's Office, "Governor Receives Creative Economy Recommendations," press release, 1 September 2004. Available at http://www.maine.gov/tools/whatsnew/index.php?topic=Gov+News&id=3169&v=Article (as of April 14, 2006).

Maine Governor's Office, "Governor Delivers State of the State Address," press release, 25 January 2005. Available at http://www.maine.gov/tools/whatsnew/index.php?topic=Gov+News&id=5168&v=Article (as of April 14, 2006).

Maine Senate, Office of the President, "Senate President Edmonds Requests Creative Economy Bond Issue," press release, 18 February 2005.

Mark, Charles Christopher, *Reluctant Bureaucrats: The Struggle to Establish the National Endowment for the Arts*, Dubuque, IA: Kendall/Hunt Publishing, 1991.

McBride, Julia Fabris, *The State of the Field: A Look at Statewide Arts Advocacy and Service Organizations*, Washington, D.C.: Americans for the Arts, 2005.

McCarthy, Kevin F., Arthur C. Brooks, Julia Lowell, and Laura Zakaras, *The Performing Arts in a New Era*, MR-1367-PCT, Santa Monica, CA: RAND Corporation, 2001.

McCarthy, Kevin F., Elizabeth H. Ondaatje, Laura Zakaras, and Arthur C. Brooks, *Gifts of the Muse: Reframing the Debate About the Benefits of the Arts*, MG-218-WF, Santa Monica, CA: RAND Corporation, 2005.

Minicucci, Paul, "The California Budget: How to Win All of the Battles and Still Lose the War," in A. Radich et al., eds., *Re-envisioning State Arts Agencies*, proceedings of a symposium held by the Western States Arts Federation, Denver, CO, 17–19 October 2003, pp. 47–52.

Montana Arts Council, "Mission Statement, Vision Statement, and Statutory Authorization," n.d. Available at http://www.art.state.mt.us/about/about_mission.asp (as of December 12, 2005).

Montana Arts Council, "Organizational Excellence Grants: Grant Application Guidelines, FY03–04," 2002. Available at http://www.art.state.mt.us/orgs/orgs_excellence.asp (as of December 12, 2004).

Montana Arts Council, "Montana Cultural Trust Application," February 2004. Available at http://www.art.state.mt.us/orgs/orgs_ca.asp (as of December 12, 2004).

Montana Arts Council, *Montana, The Land of Creativity*, Helena, MT: Montana Arts Council, January 2005.

Montana State Legislature, *Montana Code Annotated 2005*, Title 22, Chapter 2, Part 1. Available at Website maintained by the Legislative Services Division, State of Montana: http://data.opi.state.mt.us/bills/mca_toc/22_2_1.htm (as of April 14, 2006).

Moore, Mark H., *Creating Public Value: Strategic Management in Government*, Cambridge, MA: Harvard University Press, 1995.

Moore, Mark H., and Galen Williams Moore, *Creating Public Value Through State Arts Agencies*, Minneapolis, MN: Arts Midwest, 2005.

Mt. Auburn Associates, Inc., *The New Century Community Program: An Evaluation and Case Study of State Arts and Cultural Policy*, final report, Cambridge, MA: Mt. Auburn Associates, August 2002.

Mulcahy, Kevin V., "The Public Interest in Public Culture," *The Journal of Arts Management and Law*, Vol. 21, No. 1, Spring 1991, pp. 5–27.

Mulcahy, Kevin V., "The Public Interest and Arts Policy," in K. Mulcahy and M. J. Wyszomirski, eds., *America's Commitment to Culture: Government and the Arts*, Boulder, CO: Westview Press, 1995.

Mulcahy, Kevin V., "The State Arts Agency: An Overview of Cultural Federalism in the United States," *The Journal of Arts Management, Law, and Society*, Vol. 32, No. 1, Spring 2002, pp. 67–80.

National Academy of Public Administration, *National Science Foundation: Governance and Management for the Future*, a report by a panel of the National Academy of Public Administration for the United States Congress and National Science Foundation, Washington, D.C.: NAPA, April 2004.

National Assembly of State Arts Agencies (NASAA), *1991 State Arts Agency Profile*, Washington, D.C.: NASAA, 1992a.

National Assembly of State Arts Agencies (NASAA), *The State of the State Arts Agencies 1992*, Washington, D.C.: NASAA, 1992b.

National Assembly of State Arts Agencies (NASAA), *Decentralization Strategies in State Arts Agencies: Profile Breakout*, Washington, D.C.: NASAA, August 1995.

National Assembly of State Arts Agencies (NASAA), *Public Funding Sourcebook*, Washington, D.C.: NASAA, 2000a.

National Assembly of State Arts Agencies (NASAA), "Forty Action Strategies," *The NASAA Advocate*, Vol. 5, No. 4, 2000b.

National Assembly of State Arts Agencies (NASAA), "State Arts Agency Staffing Trends," *Research Briefs*, Vol. 2, No. 1, 2001.

National Assembly of State Arts Agencies (NASAA), *FY 2004 Legislative Appropriations Survey*, Washington, D.C.: NASAA, 2003a.

National Assembly of State Arts Agencies (NASAA), "Building Political Clout for the Arts," *The NASAA Advocate*, Vol. 7, No. 1, 2003b.

National Assembly of State Arts Agencies (NASAA), *FY 2005 Legislative Appropriations Survey*, Washington, D.C.: NASAA, 2005.

National Association of State Budget Officers (NASBO), *1989 State Expenditure Report*, Washington, D.C.: NASBO, 1990.

National Association of State Budget Officers (NASBO), *Budget Stability: A Policy Framework for States*, Washington, D.C.: NASBO, 1995.

National Association of State Budget Officers (NASBO), *2004 State Expenditure Report*, Washington, D.C.: NASBO, 2006.

National Conference of State Legislatures (NCSL), "Arts and the States: A Report of the NCSL Arts Task Force," Denver, CO: NCSL, 1981.

National Conference of State Legislatures (NCSL), *Mandate Monitor*, Vol. 1, No. 1 (revised), 31 March 2004.

National Conference of State Legislatures (NCSL), "State Tax and Expenditure Limits—2005," 2005a. Available at http://www.ncsl.org/programs/fiscal/tels2005.htm#tradl (as of March 17, 2006).

National Conference of State Legislatures (NCSL), "Legislative Term Limits: An Overview," 2005b. Available at http://www.ncsl.org/programs/legman/ABOUT/Termlimit.htm (as of March 17, 2006).

National Endowment for the Arts (NEA), *Annual Report*, Washington, D.C.: NEA, 1973–2004.

National Endowment for the Arts (NEA), *State Arts Agencies in 1974: Present and Accounted For*, NEA Research Division Report No. 8, Washington, D.C.: NEA, April 1978.

National Endowment for the Arts and National Assembly of State Arts Agencies (NEA/ NASAA), *State Arts Agency Funding and Grantmaking, 2001*, Washington, D.C.: NEA and NASAA, February 2003.

National Endowment for the Arts and National Assembly of State Arts Agencies (NEA/ NASAA), *State Arts Agency Funding and Grantmaking, 2003*, Washington, D.C.: NEA and NASAA, March 2003.

National Research Center of the Arts, Inc. (NRCA), *Study of State Arts Agencies: A Comprehensive Report*, New York: NRCA, 1976.

National Trust for Historic Preservation, "11 Most Endangered Places: Virginia City, Montana." Available at http://www.nationaltrust.org/11most/list.asp?i=78 (as of March 17, 2006; information last updated January 2003).

Netzer, Dick, *The Subsidized Muse: Public Support for the Arts in the United States*, Cambridge, UK: Cambridge University Press, 1978.

New Jersey State Council on the Arts (NJSCA), "Programs and Services: Overview." Available at http://www.njartscouncil.org/program1.html (as of March 17, 2006).

Nichols, Bonnie, "Demographic Characteristics of Arts Attendance, 2002," NEA Note No. 82, July 2003.

Niemeyer, Kristi, "Arts Administrator Explores the Australian Arts Scene," *State of the Arts Newspaper*, Montana Arts Council, January/February 2006.

North Carolina Arts Council, *Strategic Plan 2005–2009*, March 2005. Available at http:// www.ncarts.org/freeform_scrn_template.cfm?ffscrn_id=24 (as of March 17, 2006).

Ohio Arts Council, "Other Programs and Services," n.d. Available at http://www.oac.state. oh.us/grantsprogs/OtherPrograms.asp (as of March 17, 2006).

Ohio Arts Council, *State of the Arts Report: A Blueprint for Ohio's Communities*, Columbus, OH: Ohio Arts Council, 2001. Available at http://www.ohiosoar.org (as of March 17, 2006).

Ohio Arts Council, *Guidelines 2006/2007*. Available at http://www.oac.state.oh.us/ grantsprogs/guidelines/StaticPages/CompleteGuidelines.pdf (as of March 17, 2006).

Osborne, David, and Ted Gaebler, *Reinventing Government: How the Entrepreneurial Spirit Is Transforming the Public Sector*, Reading, MA: Addison-Wesley, 1992.

Pankratz, David B., and Carla Hanzal, "Leadership and the NEA: The Roles of the Chairperson and the National Council on the Arts," in K. Mulcahy and M.J. Wyszomirski, eds., *America's Commitment to Culture: Government and the Arts*, Boulder, CO: Westview Press, 1995.

Pennsylvania Council on the Arts, "PA Arts Council Among Government's 'Best and Brightest,'" Commonwealth of Pennsylvania news release, 29 January 2004.

Peters, B. Guy, *The Future of Governing*, 2nd edition, revised, Lawrence, KS: University Press of Kansas, 2001.

Petracca, Mark P., *The Politics of Interests: Interest Groups Transformed*, Boulder, CO: Westview Press, 1992.

Pettit, Becky, and Paul J. DiMaggio, "Public Sentiments Towards the Arts: A Critical Reanalysis of 13 Opinion Surveys," Center for Arts and Cultural Policy Studies Working Paper No. 5, Princeton, NJ: Princeton University, August 1997.

Radich, Anthony, ed., *Re-envisioning State Arts Agencies*, proceedings of a symposium held by the Western State Arts Federation, Denver, CO, 17–19 October 2003.

Sabulis, Tom, "Audit Puts Rural, Urban Areas at Odds," *Atlanta Journal-Constitution*, 5 May 2004.

Savage, James D., "Populism, Decentralization, and Arts Policy in California," *Administration and Society*, Vol. 20, No. 4, February 1989, pp. 446–464.

Schulman, Martin, "The Audience for Arts Advocacy: Building a Political Constituency," *Theatre Management Journal*, Vol. 1, No. 1, December 1997.

Schuster, J. Mark, ed., *Mapping State Cultural Policy: The State of Washington*, Cultural Policy Center of The University of Chicago, Chicago, IL: The University of Chicago, 2001.

Scott, Mel, "Government and the Arts: The Federal-State Partnership in the Arts," *Public Administration Review*, July–August 1970, pp. 376–386.

Scott, Mel, *The States and the Arts: The California Arts Commission and the Emerging Federal-State Partnership*, Berkeley, CA: Institute of Governmental Studies, University of California, Berkeley, 1971.

Snell, Ronald K., Corina Eckl, and Graham Williams, "State Spending in the 1990s," NCSL Fiscal Affairs Program, 14 July 2003. Available at http://www.ncsl.org/programs/fiscal/stspend90s.htm (as of April 14, 2006).

South Carolina Arts Commission, *A Long Range Plan for the Arts in South Carolina, 2001–2010*, Columbia, SC: South Carolina Arts Commission, 2001.

State Arts Advocacy League (SALAA), "State Arts Advocacy League (SALAA) Survey Results," unpublished document provided by NASAA, 2000.

Thurber, James A., "Issue Advocacy and Issue Ads on the Rise in the United States," *Issues of Democracy: Electronic Journal of the U.S. Information Agency*, Vol. 3, No. 2, June 1998.

U.S. Bureau of the Census, *Statistical Abstract of the United States*, Washington, D.C.: U.S. Bureau of the Census, various years.

U.S. Congress, House Committee on Education and Labor, *Aid to Fine Arts: Hearing Before the Select Subcommittee on Education on H.R. 4172, H.R. 4174, and Related Bills to Aid the Fine Arts in the United States*, 87th Congress, 1st Session, Washington, D.C., May 15, 1961.

U.S. Congress, Senate Committee on Labor and Public Welfare, *Government and the Arts: Hearing Before a Special Subcommittee on Labor and Public Welfare on S. 741, S. 785, and S. 1250*, 87th Congress, 2nd Session, Washington, D.C., 29–31 August 1962.

University of South Carolina, Institute of Public Affairs, *South Carolina State Survey: Summary Findings for the South Carolina Arts Commission*, Columbia, SC: University of South Carolina, 2000.

Warshawski, Morrie, *Alternative Sources of Income for the Arts: Final Report for the National Endowment for the Arts*, July 1999. Available at http://www.theatreontario.org/download/ Hand5-Alternative%20Sources%20of%20Income.pdf (as of March 17, 2006).

Weaver, Mary L., "The Politics of Congressional Arts Policy: National Decisions, Local Needs, and the Public Interest," in M.J. Wyszomirski, ed., *Congress and the Arts: A Precarious Alliance?* New York: ACA Books, 1988.

Western States Arts Federation (WESTAF), *State Arts Agency Governing Boards: A Review of Selected Issues*, Denver, CO: WESTAF, August 2000.

Williams, Pat, "The State of the States," in A. Radich et al., eds., *Re-envisioning State Arts Agencies*, proceedings of a symposium held by the Western States Arts Federation, Denver, CO, 17–19 October 2003, pp. 1–9.

Wilson, Alden, "Maine Arts and Culture: The Emergence of a New Force," in R. Barringer, ed., *Changing Maine, 1960–2010*, Gardiner, ME: Tilbury House, 2004, pp. 237–256.

Wilson, James Q., *Bureaucracy: What Government Agencies Do and Why They Do It*, New York: Basic Books, 1989.

Wilson, Woodrow, "The Study of Administration," *Political Science Quarterly*, Vol. 2, 1887, pp. 197–222.

Wolf, Thomas, *Managing a Nonprofit Organization in the Twenty-First Century*, New York: Simon and Schuster, 1999.

Wyszomirski, Margaret Jane, "Budgetary Politics and Legislative Support: The Arts in Congress," in M.J. Wyszomirski, ed., *Congress and the Arts: A Precarious Alliance?* New York: ACA Books, 1988.

Wyszomirski, Margaret Jane, "From Accord to Discord: Arts Policy During and After the Culture Wars," in K. Mulcahy and M.J. Wyszomirski, eds., *America's Commitment to Culture: Government and the Arts*, Boulder, CO: Westview Press, 1995.

Yee, Adelia, "The Role of Legislative Caucuses in Arts Advocacy," unpublished paper prepared for the Western States Arts Federation, October 2001.

Yeoman, Barry, "Statehouses Drop the Other Shoe," *The Nation*, 25 December 1995.

Zeigler, Joseph Wesley, *Arts in Crisis: The National Endowment for the Arts Versus America*, Chicago, IL: A Capella Books, 1994.